SOLUTIONS MANUAL

Suzanne Bell
West Virginia University

FORENSIC CHEMISTRY

Suzanne Bell

PEARSON
Prentice
Hall

Upper Saddle River, NJ 07458

Project Manager: Kristen Kaiser
Executive Editor: Nicole Folchetti
Editor-in-Chief: Dan Kaveney
Executive Managing Editor: Kathleen Schiaparelli
Assistant Managing Editor: Karen Bosch
Production Editor: Amanda Phillips
Supplement Cover Manager: Paul Gourhan
Supplement Cover Designer: Joanne Alexandris
Cover Image Credit: Shi Chen
Manufacturing Buyer: Ilene Kahn
Manufacturing Manafer: Alexis Heydt-Long

Printed in the United States of America

10 9 8 7 6 5 4 3 2 1

ISBN 0-13-185659-6

Pearson Education Ltd., *London*
Pearson Education Australia Pty. Ltd., *Sydney*
Pearson Education Singapore, Pte. Ltd.
Pearson Education North Asia Ltd., *Hong Kong*
Pearson Education Canada, Inc., *Toronto*
Pearson Educación de Mexico, S.A. de C.V.
Pearson Education—Japan, *Tokyo*
Pearson Education Malaysia, Pte. Ltd.

■ TABLE OF CONTENTS■

Solutions Manual
Forensic Chemistry
1st edition

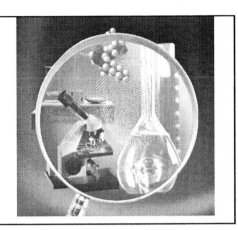

This solutions guide accompanies the first edition of the text. For the instructor, this manual should help clarify concepts and principals as applied in the homework. For the student, this manual should be *the last book opened*. Why? In my experience, students tend to use the solutions manual in a less than optimal way. For example, here is the wrong way to use a solutions manual:

1. Obtain the assigned homework from the instructor.
2. Open the solutions manual and copy the results for each problem, cleverly altering them so that it does not appear that you in fact used the solutions manual.*
3. Quit.
4. When test time comes around, study the solutions manual and hope to survive.

This is not learning, this is jockeying to do well on a test. Now, here is the correct way to use the solutions manual:

1. Obtain the assignment, also doing extra problems that are similar to those assigned.
2. Work the problem, making sure to reinforce concepts as you go. For example, if the problem involves an acid/base extraction, refer back to that section of the text and refresh your memory.
3. Check and honestly critique your work; focus on "honestly."
4. Do the next problem.
5. When finished with the assignment and related problems, open the solutions manual.
6. Check your work.
7. Close the solutions manual and put it far away from you.

---

* FYI, you are kidding yourself if you think this works.

8. Redo the problems you missed.

9. Return to step 4 and repeat.

10. When test time comes, you are ready.

A couple of other things to note: There are some corrections made here to questions in the text; they are few and minor, but nonetheless important. Also, frequent mention is made of the following references; they are abbreviated within:

"Clarke's Handbook" refers to:

Galichet, L. Y., et al., ed. *Clarke's Analysis of Drugs and Poisons,* Vol 1. and Vol. 2 London: Pharmaceutical Press, 2004. (Volume 2 contains monograms on the individual drugs and is referenced most frequently.)

PDR refers to:

Physician's Desk Reference, 58th ed. Montvale, NJ: Thomson PDR, 2004.

Physicians' Desk Reference for Nonprescription Drugs and Dietary Supplements, 22nd ed. Montvale, NJ: Medical Economics—Thomson Healthcare, 2001.

CRC Handbook refers to:

Handbook of Chemistry and Physics. 84th ed. Boca Raton, FL: CRC Press, 2003–2004.

Merck refers to:

O'Neil, M. J., et al., ed. *The Merck Index: An Encyclopedia of Chemicals, Drugs, and Biologicals.* Whitehouse Station, NJ: Merck Research Laboratories—Merck and Co., 2001.

<table>
<tr><td>

Introduction

</td><td>

CHAPTER

1

</td></tr>
</table>

From the chapter

1. Compare and contrast the adversarial system and the scientific method. List the strengths and weaknesses of both in the context of criminal and civil law.

The scientific method is based on experiment and observation, postulations of relationships, iterative testing, and drawing conclusions based on the results. The adversarial system is based on arguments from opposing parties. The scientific method does not by design pit one side against another. Certainly, there are arguments in science, but the arguments are resolved by experiment and observation. The process may take decades, but if the data is consistent and reproducible, conclusions are drawn and consensus is reached. Adversaries argue based on differing viewpoints, interpretations, and agendas. Science can be used to support or refute interpretations of events and evidence, but the outcome depends on the strength of the argument and the skill of those making it.

The adversarial system is well-suited to situations in which social and human (for lack of a better term) issues are involved. A person may have committed murder, but the reasons and circumstances are critical to the deliberation. Science, on the other hand, seeks to elucidate natural laws and to apply them to derive new knowledge. Ideally, there is no social element; gravity does not take into account mitigating circumstances, for example. This process is essential for understanding the laws of the universe since consistency and reproducibility are required to derive them. It is not an ideal system for dealing with human beings.

2. During a *Daubert* hearing, what entity ultimately decides on admissibility?

The judge, who acts as the gatekeeper.

3. What role does peer review play in science and in the law? Compare and contrast.

Argument before a judge, jury, or lawyers is loosely analogous to peer review. The appeals process could also be placed in the category since professionals of the law review the work done by other professionals. Peer review is more obvious and central in science where it is an integral part of the dissemination process. Scientific findings are submitted to peer-reviewed journals where editors assign qualified reviewers to comment on and judge the work. They may accept it as is, request more information or work, or recommend that it not be published. Publication in a peer-reviewed journal is validation of acceptance by those with similar skills, background, and understanding of the mechanism of science; materials published in non-peer-reviewed journals or sources generally are not given the same weight or credibility as peer-reviewed data.

4. Describe how a preponderance of inclusive circumstantial evidence can become conclusive in the eyes of a jury.

The Wayne Williams case is the perfect example of this phenomenon. Had a few dog hairs been found on victims, that would place under suspicion only those people who owned or might have come in contact with dogs, a large percentage of the population. It was the unique combination of hairs and fibers that was compelling. Consider your own home. What types of hairs and fibers would be found there? How would that compare with a friend's environment? You might both have the same blue carpet if you live in the same apartment building or dorm, but the hairs to be found in your two rooms would be different, as would fibers from clothing and articles of furniture. Link enough of such observations together and it becomes clear that your apartment is a much different environment than even one next door.

Integrative

1. A great scientist can still be a terrible forensic scientist; a person who gives wonderful testimony can be a terrible forensic scientist. Comment on these observations and the implication for forensic chemistry.

Forensic science and forensic chemistry require understanding and skills in comparison. It is not always an easy skill to acquire nor is the forensic mindset necessarily a natural one. In addition, a forensic scientist must be able to apply advanced techniques and knowledge to the analysis of evidence, yet present the results clearly and concisely to an audience without a comparable body of knowledge or experience. Thus, forensic scientists must be good communicators and good teachers. A great research scientist might be able to communicate with peers, but may struggle to distill the complexities of his or her work such that anyone with a high school education could grasp the concepts. Conversely, a person may be able to concisely and brilliantly present findings that are completely wrong; the skill of the presentation coupled with the audience's lack of background can result in acceptance of incorrect information. A forensic chemist must be the master of the chemistry and of the forensic aspects—to speak the truth (derived from science) in the public forum.

2. Can jurors ask questions of expert witnesses? Comment on your findings regarding this issue.

Except under rare circumstances, they cannot. They also are not usually allowed to take notes; however, practices are changing in some states. For example, in Arizona, jurors may submit questions for expert witnesses to the judge, who screens the questions and then will ask those that are probative and appropriate. In some cases, jurors are also allowed to take notes and to take these notes into deliberation.

How jurors interact with expert witnesses and how scientific evidence is presented is becoming an increasingly difficult issue, given the complexity of scientific testimony. Complicating this issue is the general lack of scientific background in jurors, judges, and lawyers. It is hard to imagine reforms not occurring as the complexity of testimony continually increases.

Food for thought

1. Is the analysis of drugs using instruments such as mass spectrometers and infrared spectrometry based on comparison?

Arguably yes. Identifications are made by comparing data to that stored in a library.

2. How important is the way in which scientific evidence is presented? Comment on the relative importance of content versus presentation. Why is learning how to testify such an important skill?

See Integrative question #1 above. A forensic scientist must be able to communicate findings concisely and clearly to the court so the trier-of-fact can properly weigh the information. Poorly communicated evidence can be as damaging as poor scientific practice.

Statistics, Sampling, and Data Quality	CHAPTER 2

From the chapter

1. A standard of Pb^{2+} for a gunshot residue analysis using atomic absorption is prepared by first dissolving 1.0390 g dried $Pb(NO_3)_2$ in distilled water containing 1% nitric acid. The solution is brought to volume in a class A 500 mL volumetric flask with an uncertainty of +/- 0.20 mL. This solution is diluted 1/10 by taking 10 mL (via an Eppendorf pipette, tolerance +/- 1.3 uL) and diluting this in 1% nitric acid to a final volume of 100 mL in a volumetric flask with a tolerance of +/- 0.08 mL. The balance has an uncertainty of +/- 0.0002 g.

a) Using conventional rounding rules, calculate the concentration of the final solution in ppm of Pb^{2+}.

The calculations should be done together and the results rounded at the end. The only exception to this is with the formula weight for the lead nitrate, which is rounded separately as an addition/subtraction. Using the periodic table in the textbook:

Formula weight of $Pb(NO_3)_2 = 207.2 + (2 \times 14.01) + (2 \times 3 \times 16.) = 331.22$

For this calculation, using this periodic table is a problem since the formula weight will needlessly limit the number of significant figures. Thus, a periodic table with more reported digits is needed, even though Pb will remain as is. The new calculation:

Formula weight of $Pb(NO_3)_2 = 207.2 + (2 \times 14.00674) + (6 \times 15.9994) = 331.2$

To obtain the concentration in ppm (mg/L), the molarity is calculated and then converted to the final value. Note that the moles of Pb in the sample are equal to the moles of $Pb(NO_3)_2$ since there is a 1:1 mole ratio of lead in lead nitrate:

$$\frac{\left[\dfrac{\left[1.0390\text{g Pb}(NO_3)_2\right]}{331.2\dfrac{g}{mole}Pb(NO_3)_2}\right]\left[\dfrac{1\text{ mole Pb}}{1\text{ mole Pb}(NO_3)_2}\right]\left[207.2\dfrac{g}{mole}Pb * \dfrac{1000\text{ mg}}{g}\right]}{0.5000\text{ L}}$$

molarity (moles/L) → ppm (mg/L

= 130.0 ppm

The result is rounded to four significant figures, the least number present in any of the measured values.

b) Determine the absolute and relative uncertainties of each value. Select the largest and report the results as a concentration range.

An easy way to visualize the largest uncertainty at a glance is to convert each one to a "1 part per" expression. For the balance:

$$\frac{0.0002g}{1.0390g} = \frac{\dfrac{0.0002}{0.0002}}{\dfrac{1.0390}{0.0002}} = \frac{1}{5195}$$

or 1 part per 5195 parts. Notice that this value is unitless.

Use the same approach to obtain the relative uncertainties of the other tools:

500 mL volumetric flask = 1 part per 2500 parts

10.00 mL transfer = 7692 parts (remember to convert uL to mL)

100 mL volumetric flask = 1 part per 1250 parts

The largest value will dominate the calculation of uncertainty and here that value is the uncertainty attributed to the 100 mL volumetric flask, 1 part in 1250 parts. As a percentage, this is (1/1250) *100 or 0.080%, also unit-independent. Therefore, the uncertainty of the final concentration can be calculated two ways:

130.0./1250 = 0.104 (1 part in 1250 parts, same relative uncertainty as the limiting value from the 100 mL volumetric flask).

-or-

130.0 * (0.00080 from the percentage) = 0.104.

The concentration in ppm using this method of calculating the uncertainty is 130.0 ppm +/- 0.1 ppm or 129.9-130.1. ppm.

c) Report the result as a range by the propagation of error method.

This is accomplished by taking the individual relative uncertainties (unitless) as calculated above and combining them as per equation 2.1:

$$e^2 = \sqrt{\left(\text{uncert.balance}\right)^2 + \left(\text{500mL flask}\right)^2 + \left(\text{Eppendorf}\right)^2 + \left(\text{100ml flask}\right)^2}$$

$$e^2 = \sqrt{\left(\frac{0.0002}{1.0390}\right)^2 + \left(\frac{0.02}{500.00}\right)^2 + \left(\frac{0.0013}{10.00}\right)^2 + \left(\frac{0.08}{100.00}\right)^2}$$

Notice that units will cancel out so that the uL uncertainty attributed to the Eppendorf pipette, 1.3 uL, is converted to mL. Solving for the error e yields 8.3 x 10^{-4} or 0.0834%. This result is close to that we obtained using the largest uncertainty as in part b, but as expected, the value is slightly larger when all uncertainties are taken into account. As a result, the uncertainty in ppm is slightly larger:

131.0. * 0.000834 = 0.109

However, with rounding, the reported range is the same as in part b.

d) Comment on your findings and why this case is somewhat unique.

As mentioned in the text, lead is one of the few elements with a molecular weight generally reported to only one decimal place. Therefore, this weight may limit significant figures in some calculations. In addition, the value for oxygen is also reported to one decimal, 16.0, in the table included in this book. However, additional decimals can be obtained using other tables. This is generally not the case with lead.

2. If an outlier is on the low side of the mean as in the example in the chapter, could a one-tailed table be used?

A one-tailed table is used when the method would always give a higher value than expected, a concentration for example. In this case, the potential outlier is on the low side of the mean and therefore a one-tailed table would not be appropriate.

3. Find the following reference for Q value tables:

Rorabacher, D. B. "Statistical Treatment for Rejection of Deviant Values: Critical Values of Dixon's "Q" Parameter and Related Subrange Ratios at the 95% Confidence Level." *Analytical Chemistry*, **63 1991, 139–148. For the trainee, determine what the %cocaine would have to be in the 11th sample for it to be eliminated at the following significance levels: 0.20, 0.10, 0.05, 0.04, 0.02, and 0.01. Present graphically and comment on the findings.**

This problem can be addressed using Excel® and by realizing that the result will be a range rather than a single value. The data is first summarized and the Q values obtained from the reference, which calls for careful reading of the text and the scenarios described. Here, we wish to find out what a single outlier value will be at either end of the distributed values, with no other outliers of concern. Therefore, the single outlier test and table, designated r_{10} in the paper, is appropriate (p. 141). This directs us to the proper table found on page 142, Table 1. The value of n will be 11 with one more included, so the corresponding table values (Q_{table}) are:

CI = 80%	90%	95%	96%	98%	99%
0.332	0.392	0.444	0.460	0.502	0.542

An outlier will be rejected if $Q_{calc} > Q_{table}$, so the next step is to determine what outlier values, when plugged into the calculation of Q (equation 2.8), will result in a Q_{calc} that just equals Q_{table}. As shown in Figure 2.5, when the data is arranged from low to high, the lowest value is 11.5% and the highest value is 15.0%. Taking the 80% interval (p = 0.20), the calculations are:

$$\frac{[11.5 - x]}{[15.0 - x]} = 0.332$$

$$11.5 - x = 0.332[15.0 - x]$$

$$11.5 - x = 4.98 - 0.0322x$$

$$6.52 - x = -0.332x$$

$$6.52 = 0.668x$$

$$x = 9.76\%$$

where [11.5 – x] represents the gap and [15.0 – x] represents the range. To simplify later calculations, this calculation can be solved generically:

$$\frac{[low - x]}{[high - x]} = Q_T$$

$$low - x = Q_T high - Q_T x$$

$$low - Q_T high = x - Q_T x$$

$$low - Q_T high = x(1 - Q_T)$$

$$x = \frac{low - Q_T high}{1 - Q_T}$$

Substituting the values of 11.5 for low, 15.0 for high, and 0.332 for Q_T yields a value of 9.76, confirming the calculation above.

To calculate the high end, the calculation is modified slightly where the gap is represented by [x – 15.0] and the range by [x – 11.5]. Simplifying as above, the generic expression is obtained:

$$x = \frac{high - Q_T low}{1 - Q_T}$$

For the 80% confidence interval, the high value cutoff is thus 16.74%. If the forensic chemist obtains a percentage cocaine value of greater than 16.74% or less than 9.76%, that value would be an outlier at the 80% confidence interval.

With generic equations in hand, a spreadsheet allows for quick solution and graphing of the results:

Low value:	11.5					
High value:	15.0					
CI:	80	90	95	96	98	99
Table:	*0.332*	*0.392*	*0.444*	*0.46*	*0.502*	*0.542*
Low cutoff:	9.76	9.24	8.71	8.52	7.97	7.36
High cutoff:	16.74	17.26	17.79	17.98	18.53	19.14

			Confidence interval	Cutoff low	Cutoff high	
			80	9.76	16.74	
			90	9.24	17.26	
			95	8.71	17.79	
			96	8.52	17.98	
			98	7.97	18.53	
			99	7.36	19.14	

Graphically:

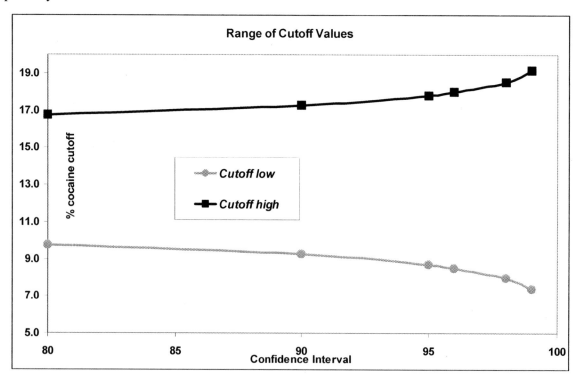

Note that as the confidence level increases, the range of values that are accepted (not classified as outliers) increases as well. To be more certain, a bigger range is required. As noted in the text, a larger range does not mean the data is "better"; in fact, the data can be less useful because the range is too large.

4. Differentiate between statistical and analytical errors.

A statistical error is one that is traceable to normal fluctuations due to random errors, which are small and equally positive and negative. An analytical error is traceable to, and due only to, laboratory procedures.

5. Justify/explain the use of the factor 3 in equation 2.13.

The factor 3 represents three standard deviations. The range of +/- 3 standard deviation units includes 99.7% of all possible outcomes, assuming that the underlying distribution is Gaussian. Refer to Figure 2.7

6. The results of equation 2.15 blatantly ignore significant figure conventions. Why?

The number is typically rounded upward to the nearest whole number. A whole number is needed when the issue is the number of samples to be taken; it makes no sense to take 13.26 samples. Furthermore, the numbers are rounded upward to be conservative. This is typical practice in forensic chemistry.

7. A large seizure arrives at the lab containing 1500 individually packaged units of a tan powder. All appear similar and each unit weighs a kilogram. This is an unusual case unlike any seen before in this facility and the lab has neither the time nor the resources to test all 1500 units.

The hint is in the wording; the lab has not seen a case like this before, so prior experience cannot be applied. The sampling plan has to be designed accordingly.

a) Design a sampling plan for qualitative analysis based on the methods described above. Summarize the outcome and justify a final value of n. As appropriate, note any assumptions made.

Since the desired analysis is qualitative, it is a yes/no or binary type of question—is the tan powder in each a controlled substance or not? The first assumption made here is that there are no particular legal constraints relative to weight, so there is no minimum number that must be shown to consist of a controlled substance to invoke different penalties. Under these assumptions, a reasonable approach is to use equation 2.20 because it is conservative:

$N = 20 + 0.10(1500 - 20) = 20 + 148 = 168$ samples tested (selected at random).

b) The recommendation is accepted and the selected subset is tested and found to contain heroin and all appear to come from the same batch. The Federal Prosecutor needs to know the average % of heroin in the seizure with an accuracy of +/-5% (relative) and a precision of +/-2%. Design a sampling plan for quantitation (if different) and defend.

The problem is more complicated now because of the need for quantitative data. Since this type of sample is new to the lab, previous experience cannot be used as information. However, with the accuracy and precision needed as known quantities, equation 2.14 could be used initially where $V_0 = 2$ (2% RSD) and $e = 5$ (5%):

$$n = \left(\frac{3 * 2\%}{5\%} \right)^2 = 1.4 \text{ or 2 samples out of the 168 tested positive}$$

While defensible on the face of it, this number is unrealistically low, particularly since the lab has not seen samples such as this before. A better approach would be to turn to data in Table 2.4; again, equation 2.20 could be used to yield a value of 35 samples.

This and similar problems point out what was emphasized in the text; there are many ways to approach representative sampling and usually (lacking concrete guidelines) more than one defensible approach. The key word is defensible.

8. A small seizure of suspected LSD is submitted to the lab and consists of 30 blotter papers.

    a) Design a sampling plan assuming that the contents of a minimum of three papers will be needed to obtain sufficient sample for presumptive and confirmatory testing.

Again, the conservative method is best reflected in equation 2.12:

$N = 20 + 1 = 21$ samples to be tested initially.

    b) After selecting n and testing, all are negative. Describe the next steps in the analysis.

Nine papers are left and some must remain in original condition, at least three. Therefore, six are available. One approach would be to test half of the remaining six, or three, samples and go from there.

    c) At what point in this LSD analysis would it be appropriate to call the results negative for LSD?

This is a difficult question and a good example of a hypothetical question. If the last three are tested and turn out negative, there is no problem and the submission does not contain LSD. If the final three are consumed and LSD is found, then there is a problem since nothing remains for others to test. This is an example where a call to the submitting office or prosecutor and consultation with supervisors and colleagues would be needed before the last of the papers are consumed.

    d) Assume that all are negative until four squares are left. Testing one gives a positive result. Note: This is an artificial and somewhat simplistic example; there are many analytical options available. This question assumes only knowledge presented so far.

Make the call and talk to others!

9. An analyst proposes a new method for the analysis of blood alcohol. As part of a method validation study, she analyzes a blind sample 5 times and obtains the following results: 0.055%, 0.054%, 0.055%, 0.052%, and 0.056%.

a) Are there outliers in the data?

We'll use the Grubbs test since it is recommended by ISO; the corresponding table values are found in Appendix 10. The questioned point is 0.052 since when the data points are arranged in order, the gap is largest between it and the nearest point:

0.052

0.054

0.055 (2)

0.056

The mean of this data set is 0.0544 and s is 0.00152:

$G = |0.052 - 0.0544| / 0.00152$ or 1.58. The G_{table} value for 4 degrees of freedom is 2.132 at the 95% CI, so the calculated value is less than the table value and the point is retained. There are no outliers.

b) Based on the results of the outlier analysis and subsequent actions, calculate the mean and %RSD of the analyst's results.

The mean and s are above; the %RSD = 2.8%.

c) If the true value of the blind sample is 0.053% +/- 0.002% (based on a range of +/- 2s), is the mean value obtained by the analyst the same as the true value at p = 0.05?

We are given a mean value for the questioned data and a way to obtain the standard deviation. If the range is +/-2s and equals 0.002%, then s = 0.001. However, lacking a value of n for the questioned result, we cannot use equation 2.11. Therefore, there are no tests described in the text that could be applied. All that can be said given the information presented is that the ranges overlap.

Integrative

1. Use the Excel function for the hypergeometric distribution to calculate the probability of selecting 5 samples that will be positive for cocaine if a seizure contains 1000 baggies and past laboratory data suggests that 50% of such recent seizures are cocaine and the rest are not. Study the results and explain how this is similar to a simple binomial distribution.

The function in Excel is called HYPGEOMDIST and the variables defined are:

Sample_s = the number of successes in the sample, here 5

Number_sample is the size of the sample, or 5

Population_s is the success rate in the population, here 50% or 500 (0.5*1000)

Number_population = 1000

Plugging in these values produces a probability of 0.03094 or 1 chance in 32 that 5 samples selected at random will all be positive for cocaine in a seizure in which half the samples are thought to be positive.

The similarity to a simple binomial is that the result is binary; either the sample is positive or it is not. The hypergeometric distribution is based on this assumption.

2. What is the difference between a confidence level and a probability?

A confidence level is the probability that a confidence interval or region will contain the true parameters. For example, a 95% confidence interval will contain the true value 95% of the time. Probability is a measure of how likely it is that some event will occur.

3. A university instructs its professors to assign grades in the range of 0.0 for an F to 4.0 for an A+. The letter grade is not recorded, only the number. When students' GPAs are calculated, they are reported with three decimal places. Can this be justified by the rules of significant figures?

No. If the professors only report grades to one decimal place, the results can only be reported to two decimal places if the last digit is included to prevent rounding error. Three decimal places cannot be kept by the normal rules of significant figures.

4. Are random samples by definition representative and vice versa? What condition must exist for this to be true?

The key assumption has to do with the nature of the sample. If it is homogeneous, then a random sample is representative and a representative sample will be random.

5. Why can there never be such a thing as a true value?

Because there is no way to know what the true value is. The only way to determine a true value is by measuring it and every measurement introduces some uncertainty. Even preparing a sample involves measurement (weighing, etc.) and so the true value can never be determined based on preparation method.

6. A government agency, the National Institute of Standards and Technology, provides certified reference materials to forensic labs. Research how the NIST certifies a reference material and comment on how this approach facilitates reliability.

An excellent reference for this appeared in a recent A-page article in the journal *Analytical Chemistry,* April 1,2005, 136A–141A. This article, entitled "Traceability of Single Element Calibration Solutions" describes the process of certifying elemental standards and how and to what these materials are traceable. The other reference is NIST itself, which maintains a terrific website with a wealth of useful information for the forensic scientist and forensic chemist. Specifically, this website defines the relevant terms as*:

*"**NIST Certified Value** - Value and its uncertainty assigned by NIST in conformance with the NIST uncertainty policy. A NIST certified value is obtained by one or more of the following measurement modes:*

1. *A definitive (or primary) method using specialized instrumentation capable of high accuracy and precision and whose errors have been thoroughly investigated and corrected; or,*

2. *Two or more independent methods at NIST using commercial instrumentation that is calibration based and with differing sources of systematic errors; or,*

3. *Interlaboratory data from selected laboratories using multiple methods and NIST SRMs as controls.*

NOTE: *The sources of error with this mode will generally result in uncertainties greater than those for the other two modes.*

NIST Noncertified Values *- Values that do not meet the criteria for NIST certified values. Such values may be referred to as **NIST reference values** or **NIST information values**.*

NOTE: *Noncertified values are often upgraded to certified values after additional measurements are performed and/or improved methodologies are applied."*

In other words, a certified value can be determined using a single analytical technique if that technique is validated and clearly understood. For the single element standards described in the *Analytical Chemistry* article, the technique used is high-performance inductively coupled plasma-optical emission spectroscopy, or HP-ICP-OES, coupled with an internal standard calibration.

7. What is the difference between a hypothetical question and a hypothesis-based question?

A hypothesis-based question is one that is stated such that a statistical significance test or hypothesis test can be applied. Examples from this chapter include the comparison of two means and the determination of outliers. Forensic chemists sometimes face hypothetical questions on the witness stand. Such questions are not answerable based on direct knowledge of the analyst. Such questions are often designed such that the analyst must offer a hypothesis to answer a question, but not in the statistical sense.

Food for thought

1. If a lab receives a case containing 100 baggies of white powder, why not cut to the chase and test all of them?

Testing all 100 baggies would not be in the interest of saving time and money. In addition, analyzing all of the data produced would consume even more valuable time. A good sampling plan would take some time, but the overall benefits would far outweigh the cost of sampling all of the baggies.

Multivariate Statistics, Calibration, and Quality Control

CHAPTER 3

From the chapter

1. Provide definitions for reliability and utility of chemical data that could be presented on the witness stand. Why are both considered part of QA?

The reliability of data is a measure of the trustworthiness of it. The quantities used to gauge reliability are accuracy and precision and reliable data is the product of comprehensive QA/QC. The utility of the data is how useful it is and how well it answers the question at hand. Data that is useful must be reliable, but reliable data may not be useful. It depends on the context. For example, a forensic chemist may produce a reliable analysis of fiber showing that it is mercerized cotton, but if the question was related to the length of the thread, this information is not useful.

2. A micropipette is certified by the manufacturer at 50.0μL TD, +/- 1.5% (95% confidence) An analyst performs a routine calibration check by pipeting a series of 5 aliquots of DI water into a tared vial. The water is at a temperature of 25.0°C. The following data is obtained:

n	Weight (cumulative), g
1	0.0494
2	0.0997
3	0.1484
4	0.1985
5	0.2477

Is the micropipette performing according to specs? Cite sources.

First calculate the range of acceptable performance as 1.5% of 50.0 or 0.75uL. The range of acceptable values is 49.2–50.8uL, recalling that 0.5 type numbers are rounded to the nearest even value. Next, units have to match, so either the weights obtained by the analyst need to be converted through density to volumes or the certified volume must be converted to weight. Since the final working unit is volume, the five weights should be converted. Using the CRC Handbook (84th Edition) values for water density, d = 0.997 g/mL. Rearranging gives v = m (g)/0.997 g mL^{-1}. At this point, a spreadsheet is useful:

n	Weight (cumulative), g	Net Wt.	Volume
1	0.0494	0.0494	49.55
2	0.0997	0.0503	50.45
3	0.1484	0.0487	48.85
4	0.1985	0.0501	50.25
5	0.2477	0.0492	49.35
Water density at 25.0°C:	**0.997**		
Volume			
Mean	49.69		
Standard Error	0.30		
Median	49.549		
Standard Deviation	0.660		
%RSD	1.3		
Sample Variance	0.436		
Range	1.60		
Count	5		
Confidence Level (95.0%)	0.82		

The weight of each trial is obtained by subtraction and then the density conversion is applied. The summary table was generated using the *Summary Statistics* tool in *Data Analysis*.

Using the 95% CI as the uncertainty, the analyst's data shows the pipette delivering 49.69uL +/- 0.82 uL or 48.9 – 50.5 uL. Because the acceptable range is 49.2–50.8uL, the performance falls within control limits. The t-test of means is not applicable here since the individual values used to generate it are not known; so, based on the material presented in the chapter, this is the best answer we can provide.

3. In complex environmental samples such as soils, spikes are used to measure the matrix effect. The range of allowable recoveries for 1,2-dichloroethane-d4, a spike compound, is 80–120%. How is it possible to obtain a recovery of greater than 100%? Hint: This happens frequently and it does not imply that this compound is in the sample.

This is an artifact of how internal standard calibration works. Recall that the ratios of the target to the internal standard are used and not the individual values for concentration or instrument response. The instrument response is calculated as the ratio of the internal standard response/target analyte response. If this ratio is too high, then the calculated concentration will be too high. If a spike of 1,2-dichloroethane-d4 is added to a sample along with the internal standard, the assumption is that the two compounds will behave identically. However, in complex matrices such as soil, this is not always the case. Suppose the internal standard response was normal, but the response for the spike was low. This would drive the ratio higher than it should be and when the calibration curve is applied, the calculated concentration would be higher than the actual. In the case of a spike, where a known amount is added, this would result in a %recovery of >100%.

4. In Figure 3.13, what two points are physically the closest? Show the calculation for the distance. Which two points are the farthest apart? Show the calculation for d.

The two points that are physically the closest are B10 and C10. The distance separating them is calculated using equation 3.3, the Euclidean distance. The values for x, y, and z are found in Table 3.1 and are [6, 16, 3.2] and [7, 15, 3.3] respectively. The calculation is:

$$d = \sqrt{[(6 - 7)^2 + (16 - 15)^2 + (3.2 - 3.3)^2]} = 1.42$$

Looking at Figure 3.13, these two points are near the left-hand side and the linkage distance between them falls at 1.42.

5. PCA is based on the assumption that variables can be linearly correlated. If this is not the case, how would this be diagnosed?

The easiest way would be to create a correlation matrix like that shown in Figure 3.7 and Table 3.2. The lack of correlations would be easily seen and verified quantitatively.

6. Does cluster analysis as described here assume a linear relationship among variables?

No, all that matters is separation of the variable in the data space, not the existence of any relationship among them.

7. Why are deuterated compounds frequently used as internal standards?

They are used because they will behave chemically identical to their nondeuterated analogs. For example, benzene-d6 is chemically identical to benzene and so the deuterated analog will behave identically through any extraction procedures. However, when an MS is used as the detector, the mass difference of 6 amu is more than enough to differentiate the two.

8. If an analyst inadvertently generates a least squared fit calibration curve that is forced through the origin, what type of error would be introduced? Would accuracy or precision be affected? What types of QA/QC samples and procedures could identify this error?

Accuracy is the closeness of a test result to an accepted reference value and precision is the reproducibility of a series of measurements under optimal conditions. Therefore, forcing the curve through the origin would affect accuracy, but not precision. Using the calibration curve that was forced through the origin would not produce a result as close to the accepted reference value as one that had not been forced through the origin. However, results obtained using the same calibration curve forced through the origin should be reproducible and therefore precise.

9. In Exhibit A, the point was made that a calibration result from the middle of a curve should never be arbitrarily thrown away. The same is not necessarily true of calibration points that define the upper and lower extremes of the curve. Why?

The points that define the lower portions of a calibration curve can be affected by the limit of quantitation of the instrument. The points that define the upper limits of the calibration curve could be affected by saturation of the sample and therefore should not be used. Points that are outliers on the linear portion of the graph should not be disregarded or eliminated because they could be indicators of a problem with the method or sample.

10. A toxicologist receives a blood sample thought to contain a low level of a new poison just identified. The quantitation is of paramount importance because the treatment, if given to a healthy person, can cause severe side-effects. What would be the best choice for calibration method based on the discussion above?

Standard addition would be the best choice, since a perfect matrix match is provided.

Integrative

1. What levels of quality assurance are there in typical freshman chemistry labs? Organic labs?

In freshman chemistry labs, the experimental procedures are typically tested by professors and others before being included in the laboratory manual. Reagents are ordered from reliable sources and the observations are often based on reliable tests (such as litmus paper) and instruments (such as analytical balances and pH meters). The same would be true for organic labs, but more sophisticated instruments (IR spectrophotometers and gas chromatographs) are used. However, these labs are rarely up to the QA standards met in forensic labs because the reagents and instruments are often not traceable and/or certified.

2. Draw a diagram that employs two Gaussian curves to illustrate the concept of bias. What does this have in common with the t-test of means introduced in the previous chapter? In what ways does it differ?

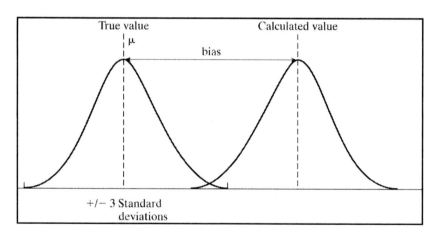

The figure illustrates bias that results from a systematic error. The true value has the expected uncertainty associated with it as does the bias. If the error is systematic, then the offset of the experimentally determined value should always have the same offset from the true value along with the normal small random errors. The t-test of means described in Chapter 2 is a hypothesis test designed to identify a true bias from an extreme, but still expected, result. However, in the case of bias, we are working within the same population, whereas with the t-test, it is not known if the population is the same; in effect, that is the question that is posed in the hypothesis and evaluated.

3. A forensic toxicologist receives a postmortem blood sample and performs a routine screening analysis followed by GCMS to confirm the presence of cocaine and its metabolites. The toxicologist also performs a quantitative analysis for these analytes. He writes his report, sends it through the lab system, and it arrives on the desk of the Medical Examiner. Identify at least three levels of peer review that would have occurred in this example. Hint: Much of the applicable peer review would have occurred off-stage and in the past.

This can be answered by revisiting Figure 3.1, which illustrates the layers of quality assurance and quality control. Within the toxicology section, there will have been peer review by his supervisor, peers, and QA officer. The laboratory, if accredited, and the analyst, if certified, will have undergone an extensive peer review process. The validated analytical method by definition will have been reviewed in the literature and within the laboratory.

4. Obtain the following reference: Gardner, W. P., et al. "Application of Quantitative Chemometric Analysis Techniques to Direct Sampling Mass Spectrometry." *Analytical Chemistry* **73 (2001), 596–605. Using Table 1 as the input, perform a principal components analysis. Can the dimensionality of this data be reduced using this technique?**

The data table includes calibration and prediction data as is common when a model is to be constructed and then tested. With PCA, the goal is to reduce the dimensionality of all data and so for this PCA, all instances were used. The program used was *Statistica* (Statsoft, Tulsa OK), but any number of programs can be used,

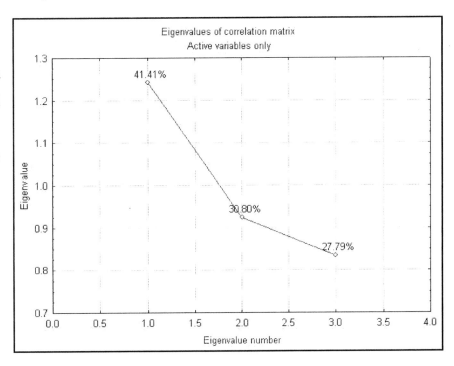

including add-ons available for Excel® (although PCA is a standard part of the spreadsheet program). Once the data is entered, PCA is applied with the results summarized in the figure shown above. The dataset contains three variables, the first two principal components account for about 72% of the variance. [†]Thus, this dataset is not a good candidate for reduction using PCA since a large amount of variance (about 28%) in the data would not be captured.

5. Research how the NIST is able to apply the label "certified" and "standard" to CRM and SRMs. What particular step is crucial and why does it lend such authority? Discuss this in terms of error types as well as in terms of accuracy and precision.

The NIST maintains a terrific website with a wealth of useful information for the forensic scientist and forensic chemist. Specifically, this website defines the relevant terms as*:

*"**NIST Certified Value** - Value and its uncertainty assigned by NIST in conformance with the NIST uncertainty policy. A NIST certified value is obtained by one or more of the following measurement modes:*

1. *A definitive (or primary) method using specialized instrumentation capable of high accuracy and precision and whose errors have been thoroughly investigated and corrected; or,*

2. *Two or more independent methods at NIST using commercial instrumentation that is calibration based and with differing sources of systematic errors; or,*

3. *Interlaboratory data from selected laboratories using multiple methods and NIST SRMs as controls.*

NOTE: *The sources of error with this mode will generally result in uncertainties greater than those for the other two modes.*

NIST Noncertified Values *- Values that do not meet the criteria for NIST certified values. Such values may be referred to as **NIST reference values** or **NIST information values**.*

NOTE: *Noncertified values are often upgraded to certified values after additional measurements are performed and/or improved methodologies are applied."*

*Source: National Institute of Standards and Technology, US Department of Commerce. Available on-line, URL: http://ts.nist.gov/ts/htdocs/230/232/ABOUT/program_info.htm Downloaded April 18, 2005.

The key is the use of an extremely accurate, precise, and validated primary analytical method or two independent methods. Also important is the interlaboratory comparison.

[†] Note that the Eigenvalue is shown here; this value is produced as a result of the statistical analysis. The interested reader can consult a book on multivariate statistics or chemometrics for more information on the details of PCA.

6. Deuterated compounds are useful as internal standards, while isotopes such as ^{14}C or tritium are not. Why?

Tritium and ^{14}C are radioactive (unstable) compared with deuterium, which is a stable isotope.

7. The following data is produced as part of a laboratory accreditation check sample. Critique the results. "[]" is the concentration ratio.

ppb codeine	Peak area	ppb IS	Peak area	[] ratio	area ratio
15.0	9599	50.0	29933	0.30	0.32
35.0	21456	50.0	30099	0.70	0.71
75.0	45326	50.0	32051	1.50	1.41
125.0	82100	50.0	32912	2.50	2.49
150.0	95003	50.0	31100	3.00	3.05
200.0	122409	50.0	30303	4.00	4.04
Blank:	3100	50.0	31954		
Known (100.0 +/- 1.0ppb):	51208	50.0	33000		
Cal check (Independent, 125.0 +/-0.1 ppb):	74912	50.0	32844		

To critique, first determine the concentrations of the blankc, known, and calibration check solution using the data provided and your knowledge of internal standards. This requires the equation of the calibration curve as well as a graph:

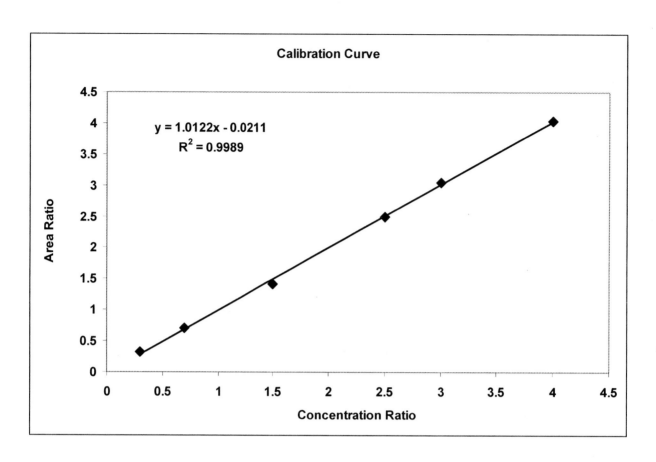

The equation of the calibration curve is $y = 1.0122x - 0.0211$ where x is the concentration ratio and y is the response ratio. We are solving for the concentration, so first solve for y and then multiply it by the concentration of the internal standard, here 50.0 ppb. The results are summarized below, again using a spreadsheet:

	Area ratio	Concentration	%Error
Blank:	0.10	3.9	NA
Known (100.0 +/- 1.0ppb):	1.55	77.5	-22.5
Cal check (Independent, 125.0 +/-0.1 ppb):	2.28	114.4	-8.5

Now we have the information needed for a critique. First, the curve has an acceptaple correlation coefficient and is not showing signs of saturation or erratic behavior at the low end. The areas of the internal standard are acceptably reproducible with a %RSD of ~ 4% for the calibration runs. However, the calibration check sample analysis indicates an unacceptable negative bias of -8.5%. The blank has detectable codeine but it is less than the LOQ. If a problem, the residual would have produced a positive bias, which was not observed. Finally, the results for the known are unacceptably low. There is likely a systematic error that is causing a negative bias. A possible source is the original stock solution for the calibration.

Food for thought

1. Is there such a thing as a "true" value for the concentration of a prepared blind quality assurance sample?

No, the true value is always a range since any preparation step such as using an analytical balance will impart uncertainty.

2. Are standard desktop calculators traceable? Can a user be absolutely sure that every operation is correct, assuming that the key entry is?

They are typically not. The best way to test calculators is through a series of examples with known outcomes, but there is no systematic single standard for doing so. The user cannot ever be 100% certain of every outcome. However, if the value 100 is entered and a square root of 10 returned with this operation is requested, that instills confidence in the programmed algorithm used to determine the square root.

Sample Preparation, Thin-Layer Chromatography, and Immunoassay	CHAPTER 4

From the chapter

1. Equation 4.2 expresses the relationship exploited by breath alcohol testing that is done in the field. Why is this test not considered accurate enough to determine blood alcohol concentration? In other words, why is this considered to be a presumptive rather than conclusive test?

Field tests for blood alcohol are considered presumptive because they rely on a partitioning constant (K_H) to determine the blood alcohol level. Equilibrium constants are dependent on experimental conditions and variables such as temperature; such methods are not as accurate as those based on calibration curves.

2.

    a) Without resorting to calculations, comment on the relative solubility of the following compounds: Silver bromate $K_{sp} = 5.5 \times 10^{-5}$; silver sulfide 6×10^{-51}; magnesium carbonate 3.5×10^{-8}; $Mn(OH)_2$ 1.6×10^{-13}.

First, determine the formulas for those not given—$AgBrO_3$, Ag_2S, $MgCO_3$, and $Mn(OH)_2$—information needed to determine if the generic expression falls under the S^2 or $4S^3 = K_{sp}$ category, which is necessary in some cases. Clearly, the Ag_2S is the least soluble given the miniscule value of K_{sp}; conversely, $AgBrO_3$ is the most soluble. $MgCO_3$ is second most soluble, and $Mn(OH)_2$ is third. These conclusions are reached by examining the exponents and taking into account the root, be it a square or a cube.

    b) Give the solubility product constant in the form pK_{sp}.

To obtain a pK_{sp}, simply take the $-\log K_{sp}$. This yields:

$AgBrO_3 = -\log(5.5 \times 10^{-5}) = 4.26$

$Ag_2S = -\log(6\times10^{-51}) = 50.2$

$MgCO_3 = -\log(3.5\times10^{-8}) = 7.46$

$Mn(OH)_2 = -\log(1.6\times10^{-13}) = 12.8$

c) Calculate the solubility of each.

$AgBrO_3 : Ksp = [Ag][BrO_3] = S^2 = 5.5\times10^{-5}; \quad S = 7.4\times10^{-3}$

Similarly:

$Ag_2S = 4S^3 = 6\times10^{-51}; \quad\quad\quad\quad\quad\quad\quad S = 1.0\times10^{-17}$

$MgCO_3 = S^2 = 3.5\times10^{-8}; \quad\quad\quad\quad\quad\quad S = 1.9\times10^{-4}$

$Mn(OH)_2 = 4S^3 = 1.6\times10^{-13}; \quad\quad\quad\quad\quad S = 3.4\times10^{-5}$

Note how the calculations match the estimated solubility order from part a.

d) At what pH would manganese hydroxide precipitate out?

Since we are not given a concentration for the maganese, the answer has to be presented as an expression in which the pH and the [Mn], here expressed as pMn, are variables. First simplify the solubility expression as:

$4[Mn][OH]^2 = 1.6\times10^{-13}$ or using logarithms:

$\log(4) + \log Mn + 2\log[OH] = -12.8$ (from parts b and c above)

$\log Mn + 2\log[OH] = -13.4$

$-\log Mn - 2\log[OH] = 13.4$

$pMn + 2pOH = 13.4$

$0.5pMn + pOH = 6.7$

$0.5pMn + (14-pH) = 6.7$

$pH = 0.5pMn + 7.3$

For example, assume that the concentration of manganese in a solution is $1.0\times10^{-4}M$. If so, pMn = 4.0 and 0.5 times this value equals 2.0. The pH at which the solid hydroxide can form is calculated as 2.0 + 7.3 = 9.3

3. In question 2, what other factor(s) must be considered in the case of the carbonate and the hydroxide?

As noted, it is pH. The carbonate ion forms bicarbonate ions and participates in the carbonate buffer system; so, pH is also important here. Blood is an example of a carbonate buffer.

4.

a) Barium is a toxic metal yet is given to a patient in large quantities when x-rays of the stomach or intestines are needed. For such imaging, the patient is given a "milk shake" containing barium sulfate. Given the known toxicity, why is this safe?

This is safe because barium sulfate is nearly insoluble (Ksp = 1.1×10^{-10}); plus, we are not given information of the toxicity of the metal verses the ion.

b) Comment on the implications for the toxicology of metals such as mercury, cadmium, lead, and antimony.

There are two key factors to consider in such cases. First, how bioavailable is the toxin? The barium in $BaSO_4$ is not biologically available because it is locked in a relatively insoluble material and thus, cannot do harm. Second, the oxidation state and subsequent bonding is critical. For example, metallic mercury Hg(l) is actually one of the less toxic forms of mercury, whereas dimethyl mercury CH_3HgCH_3 with mercury in the +2 oxidation state is one of the most toxic.

5. Aspirin (acetylsalicylic acid) has a pK$_a$ of 3.5. The pH of the stomach is approximately 1 while the pH of the intestines is approximately 6. Calculate the fraction of aspirin that is ionized in each area (show work), and use the results to predict where the drug is preferentially absorbed.

To calculate the fraction of aspirin that is ionized in the stomach, the relationships presented in Figure 4.6 are used (acidic drugs). A$^-$ represents the ionized form and HA the un-ionized form:

pH = pKa + log [A$^-$]/[HA]   1 = 3.5 + log [A$^-$]/[HA]   0.0032/1 = [A$^-$]/ [HA]

Likewise, the fraction of ionization in the intestine is calculated:

6 = 3.5 + log [A$^-$]/[HA]   2.5 = log [A$^-$]/[HA]   316/1 = [A$^-$]/ [HA]

Since the drug must be in the ionized form to be absorbed into the body, the fraction of ionization is higher for the intestine and the drug will be preferentially absorbed there.

6. Repeat the calculation in Question 5 for caffeine, a weak base with a pK$_a$ of 0.6

The approach is the same except now use the relationship presented in Figure 4.7:

pH = pK$_a$ + log [un-ionized] / [ionized]

The pKa is 0.6 and so for the stomach:

1 = 0.6 + log [un-ionized] / [ionized]

The ratio is ~2.51 so about twice as much is neutral as is ionized. In the intestine, the ratio is on the order of 250,000; so, much more is neutral than ionized as expected. A base does not tend to dissociate in a basic environment or in this case, the base remains neutral in the basic environment.

7. Diazepam tablets are supplied in 2, 5, and 10 mg increments. Assume several tablets are received in a lab as evidence. Using the *Physician's Desk Reference*, the analyst was able to tentatively identify them as Valium, 10 mg. You further learn that the tablets also contain anhydrous lactose, starches, dyes, and calcium stearate. Describe a method to isolate the active ingredient from fillers using a solvent/aqueous extraction scheme. Justify and explain each step.

According to Clarke's Handbook, diazepam is a base with a pK$_a$ of 3.4. It is also soluble (1:2) in chloroform. The easy way to accomplish this separation is by a dry extraction with chloroform. Some of the dyes may also extract; depending on their nature, many could be removed by drying the original chloroform extract, re-dissolving in a buffer with a pH of ~5.4, and re-extracting in chloroform. Only the dyes that remain neutral under these conditions will transfer into this second chloroform extraction.

8. Quinine ($C_{20}H_{24}N_2O_2$) is a dibasic molecule with pK$_a$'s of 5.1 and 9.7. It is encountered as a diluent (cutting agent) for heroin. To successfully extract quinine from an aqueous solution, what pH should be used and why?

To extract into a neutral solvent from an aqueous solution, all ionization must be suppressed. Thus, focus attention on the larger pK$_a$ of 9.7. The extraction should be undertaken at a pH of ~11.7, rather than 7.1, using the pH + 2 guidelines discussed in the chapter.

9. Devise a solvent extraction method that could be used to separate a mixture of powdered sugar, cornstarch, cocaine, and amphetamine. Justify each step and separation. Repeat using SPE to affect the separation.

The challenge here will be to separate the two basic drugs from each other; in practice this would be accomplished using GC. However, for the purposes of this question, the following method is proposed for a crude separation: Place the sample in a beaker and add dilute NaOH to bring the pH to ~10 and extract with chloroform. Based on data obtained from Clark's Handbook, the pK$_a$ of cocaine is 8.6 and that of amphetamine is 10.1. At this pH, the cocaine will be mostly neutralized and extractable, while the amphetamine will remain mostly ionized and in the aqueous phase. Pouring the aqueous phase through a filter will isolate the starch and transfer the amphetamine and sugar in solution to another beaker. Now the pH can be set to ~12 and the solution extracted with chloroform to isolate the amphetamine and leave the sugar in the aqueous phase.

10. A case sample from a suspected arson fire is submitted to the lab. The fire was suppressed with large volumes of water. The exhibit submitted to the lab consists of ~50 mLs of this water. The water appears dirty and has suspended solids and other visible debris. Propose a SPE method to clean the sample and isolate any residual accelerants assuming gasoline or another hydrocarbon was used.

The matrix here is water, a polar media, and solid debris. The analytes are nonpolar or nearly nonpolar hydrocarbons and so affecting a separation should be relatively easy. One approach would be to direct the water sample onto a SPE cartridge containing a nonpolar and hydrophobic solid phase such as -C_3H_{17} (see Table 4.4). This should pass all of the water while trapping the solid debris on top of the column and the polar analytes within. The column could be further cleaned if needed using methanol or other polar solvents. To elute the nonpolar analytes, a solvent such as hexane, pentane, or carbon disulfide could be used. Note that using an octadecyl phase such as C18 would not be as good a choice because it will be very difficult to extract the non-polar analytes from it.

11. List some practical limitations of RIA.

Some practical limitations of RIA are the disposal of radioactive waste, removal of the unbound phase, and protection of the technician from radioactivity.

12. Would the enzymatic preparation of hair be classified as an extraction or a digestion?

Using enzymes digests the matrix and so the term digestion would be the more appropriate of the two.

13. Clearly differentiate between EMIT and ELISA.

The key difference is that EMIT is a homogenous assay, while ELISA is heterogeneous. In ELISA, the antibody to the drug is bound to a surface, but in EMIT, the antibody is free to move in solution.

14. Explain the patterns observed in Figure 1, Applying the Science 4.1.

The y-axis is the logP value multiplied by a constant; the smaller the value, the more water-soluble. The x-axis is a measure of water solubility as well, but of neutral compounds. The column is nonpolar and lipophilic friendly. Initially, the elution solvent in the gradient is nonpolar and so lipophilic compounds will elute relatively quickly. As the elution solvent becomes more polar, the lipophilic compounds will have a greater relative affinity for the stationary phase and will linger in the column longer. Thus, the farther to the right a point is, the more lipophilic the compound is (and also the more hydrophobic).

Integrative

1. Diazepam (Valium®) is a member of the benzodiazepine family of drugs. This drug, at one time the most prescribed drug in the country, has a single ionization center with a pK$_a$ reported as 3.4. Answer the following questions about this drug:

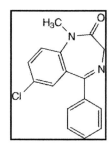

a) Draw the structure or obtain it from a reliable referenced source. Indicate the location of the ionizable center.

The nitrogen with three single bonds, one to a methyl group, is the ionization center.

Source: Clarke's Analysis of Drugs and Poisons, Volume 2, p. 897.

b) Is diazepam acidic, basic, or neutral? Justify.

It is a weak base; it has no acidic groups and a nitrogenous base site.

c) What would be the pH of a 0.01M solution of diazepam? Show your work.

The pK$_a$ (from Clarke's) is 3.3, thus the K$_a$ = 5.0x10^{-4}. Since this compound is a weak base, K$_b$ will be needed through:

K$_a$K$_b$ = 1.0x10^{-14}; K$_b$ = 2.0x10^{-11}. This value is several orders of magnitude smaller than the molarity of the diazepam and so the amount of dissociate is negligible and the quadratic equation is not necessary. The generic base dissociation equation can be used:

$B \leftarrow \rightarrow BH^+ + OH^-$

$K_b = [BH^+][OH^-] = x^2 = 2.0 \times 10^{-11}$

$x = [OH^-] = 4.5 \times 10^{-6}$; pOH = 5.35 and pH = 8.65

d) What would be an optimal pH to extract diazepam using a simple solvent extraction?

Refer to question 7 in the previous section.

2. For drugs supplied as salts, it is usually possible to determine if the drug is acidic or basic by the chemical name. Explain and provide a list of three examples not in the chapter. Hint: PDR.

By looking at the name of the drug, it is possible to determine whether it is acidic or basic. An acidic drug will need a negatively charged ion to form the salt, so chlorides or carbonates are usually indicative of acidic drugs. Conversely, basic drugs will need a positively charged ion in order to form the salt. Basic drugs will usually have names including sodium or potassium.

3. Review the list of solvents in Table 4.5 and find their MSDS sheets and comparative pricing information. Suggest which are likely and which are unlikely to be used routinely in a forensic lab based on findings.

First, eliminate the obvious: water, methanol and ethanol; all are widely used and essential to forensic chemistry. Pentane and diethyl ether are used sparingly because of their extreme volatility, which makes them difficult to work with. Carbon tetrachloride is a known carcinogen and no longer used in forensic or most other labs. This leaves:

Solvent	Cost per L	Toxicity
Pet ether	$18	low
Isooctane	$61	low
Chloroform	$42	moderate
Methylene chloride	$60	moderate–high
Ethyl acetate	$18	moderate
Acetone	$27	low
Acetonitrile	$34	high

Of course, there is toxicity associated with all, so only a relative measure is provided; costs were obtained from vendor websites, were current as of mid-2005, and were obtained for reagent grade chemicals. Methylene chloride tends to be more costly and has nearly the same solvent strength as chloroform and thus, use could be minimized. Acetonitrile use would also be discouraged, but for some applications such as HPLC, it is essential.

4. TLC plates can be made in the lab, but it is recommended that they be purchased to insure the uniformity of the solid phase thickness. Comment on the role that thickness would play and illustrate how an uneven surface would impact performance and appearance.

Thin layer chromatography relies on capillary action of the solvent up the plate to carry and separate the components of the analyte. If the thickness of the solid phase on the plate is not uniform, then the path of the components will be altered and the shape of the spot would be distorted. For those analyses where the location of the spot on the plate is of importance, the nonuniformity of the plate could affect the results.

5. For the mini-column cleanup described for LSD (lysergic acid diethylamide), suggest other combinations of solid phase and solvent that might work as well. Based on the structure and chemical character of LSD, why is the method depicted a good one?

The goal for selection of a solid phase is to slow the progress of the LSD, but not stop it so that contaminants either flow out ahead of the LSD (i.e., have less affinity for the solid phase than LSD) or are retained much longer (have higher affinity). As per Table 4.4, florisil is polar, hydrophilic due to this polarity, and slightly basic. The structure of LSD, shown in Chapter 7, is an ergot alkaloid with basic character and thus, has some affinity for the florisil, but not so much that it cannot be stripped out by excess chloroform. Appropriate solid phases for this same application might be an aminopropyl or a basic alumina phase.

6. For each of the specific immunoassay techniques, draw a generic calibration curve and indicate if the corresponding r value would be positive or negative. The key here is to understand what is being monitored; the appearance of a new product through a linked reaction or the disappearance of one. With this in mind, the calibration responses shown at right are expected.

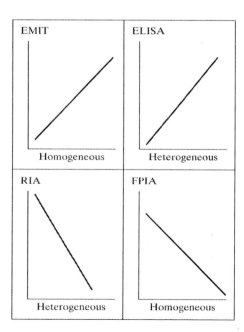

7. A relatively new type of immunoassay is based on the agglutination of coated latex particles. Research the procedure and summarize in a few figures how it works. What are some advantages and disadvantages of the technique?

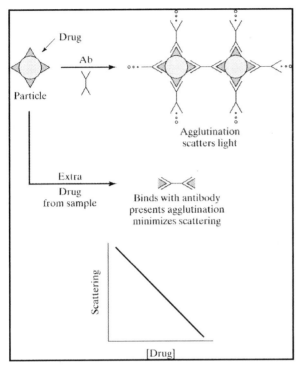

The measurement is simple; scattering is the same thing as turbidity. It is also homogenous, which also limits complexity, but makes the test more susceptible to interferences.

8. A certain drug has a K_b of 3.2×10^{-6}. What are the corresponding K_a and pK_a?

Recall that $K_w = K_a K_b$; thus
$K_a = 1.00 \times 10^{-14}/3.2 \times 10^{-6}$.
$K_a = 3.13 \times 10^{-9}$ and $pK_a = 8.5$.

9. Discuss the similarities of cation/anion exchange methods and competitive binding immunoassay techniques.

In both techniques, the analytes associate and dissociate according to concentrate and relative affinity effects.

10. When samples are extracted using SPE or related techniques, internal standards are added before the sample is placed on the column. Why?

This is done so that these compounds will experience the same conditions as the analyte compounds they are designed to track. The internal standard method relies on response ratios, but both the analyte and internal standard have to be treated the same way all through the sample preparation step to account for factors that cause a loss of analyte.

11. According to the Merck Index, a 1% solution (wt/vol) of caffeine in water produces a pH of 6.9. Calculate the K_a and pK_a of caffeine.

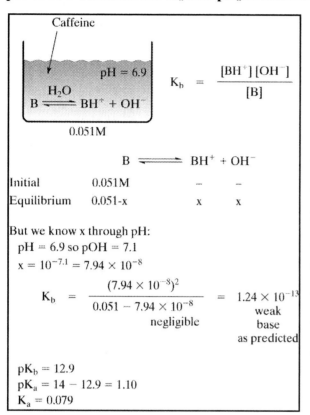

A 1% w/v solution of caffeine translates to a molarity of 0.051M. The molarity is calculated by assuming a liter of water containing 10 g of caffeine, FW 194.2. Note that the volume can be anything we select since pH is not a function of volume; so, a liter is convenient. We can also predict that caffeine is probably a relatively weak base since the pH is slightly acidic. This should not be too troubling; recall that even pure water is slightly acidic to start with due to the presence of dissolved CO_2 and the resulting carbonic acid formation and dissociation.

Food for thought

1. If a sample is analyzed using TLC with two different solid phases and several solvent systems, would the results be considered conclusive? What about inclusion of standards and several developing reagents? At what point does a string of presumptive and screening tests become conclusive?

Of course there is no definitive answer to this since it can never be known for certain how every conceivable compound will respond under a given set of experimental conditions. Adding the analysis of standards as part of any TLC experiment adds confidence to results, but not absolute certainty to an identification.

2. Related to Question 1 above, comment on the analogy between the described scenario and the situation of combining circumstantial evidence to infer a fact.

This point is reached when there is negligible likelihood that an alternative explanation can explain the facts, or in this case, experimental results. In criminal cases, the trier-of-fact reaches this conclusion with the assistance of scientific testing.

3. Immunoassay is a staple of forensic toxicology, but is rarely used in the analysis of drugs as physical evidence. Comment.

Immunoassay is designed for use with liquid or liquefied sample matrices and so is well-suited to toxicology applications. In solid dose analysis, making the solution requires an additional step and time without a benefit over TLC and presumptive tests, which work well with solid matrices.

Instrumentation

From the chapter

1. What is the best wavelength to use for examination of the smallest visible samples? Why?

An important point is to select the wavelength range such that scattering is minimized since scattered light represents lost signal and lost information. Scattering becomes a problem as the wavelength approaches the size of the particle; for the visible range, this would correlate to particles with dimensions in the range of 400 nm to 700 nm or, in terms of microns, 0.4 μm to 0.7 μm. A typical forensic microscope can distinguish particles with dimensions on the order of a micron; so at high magnification and smaller particles, bluer light is less likely to be scattered.

2. Based on the information presented in Exhibit B, explain why blue light bends more (is refracted to a larger degree) than red light.

Note the correction on reference. The difference is due to the different wavelengths, with blue having a shorter wavelength and red having a longer wavelength.

3. Draw a box diagram of a simple microscope next to that of a simple spectrophotometer. Trace the light paths and show common components and features. Based on this, how would you expect a polarizing IR microscope to function? Draw a schematic.

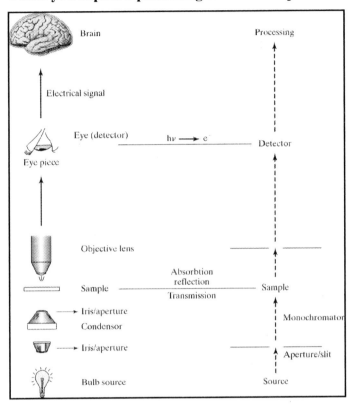

The similar components include slits and apertures to control the intensity of the light, a sample that can interact via several mechanisms, a detector that converts photons to electrical current, and a processor.

An IR microscope would look like a microscope, but have an IR source and optics that are transparent to IR radiation as opposed to visible light. Since the user will need to site and position the sample, visible light capability would be required and this is usually implemented using different objectives mounted on the nosepiece of the microscope. As in normal PLM, the analyzer and polarizer would be placed in the light path, but as with the lenses and other optics, the polarizing filters would have to be specific to IR radiation.

4. Why are fluorescent and phosphorescent emissions always "redder" than the source used to stimulate the emission?

This is because the transitions involved are between energy gaps that are closer together than the original excitation. The shorter the gap, the lower the energy and the redder the photon.

5. How would a gas phase UV spectrum of acetone compare with one obtained in the liquid phase? From a forensic point of view, would this provide any additional information or value?

The peaks would be sharper since interactions with solvents and neighboring molecules would be drastically reduced. From a forensic perspective, this increased resolution is not particularly useful since the spectrum still does not provide definitive identification.

6. If the resolution of an FTIR depends on the distance the mirror travels, why aren't relatively long moving distances such as 2 or 4 cm used? What is the tradeoff?

The tradeoff is speed. The farther the mirror has to move, the longer it will take to complete the cycle and thus, the longer it takes to scan the sample through the wavelength range. This negates one of the primary advantages of FTIR—the ability to rapidly collect and average many spectra to reduce noise.

7. Why would the electron clouds of bonds made with larger atoms be more polarizable than those from smaller atoms?

The larger the electron cloud, the farther the outer electrons are from the nucleus and the less influenced they are by the electrostatic attraction. These outer electrons are also spread out over a larger volume of space. In other words, they will be easier to move than those closer in.

8. Why can't an atomic absorption instrument be designed like a simple UV/VIS instrument where a lamp is the source and a monochromator isolates the wavelength of interest such as 589.3 for sodium?

By filtering out all other wavelengths, the intensity of the light is vanishingly small, far too small to allow for any meaningful measurements of changes in that signal, particularly when decreased by absorbance.

9. In AA, does it matter if the target atom is ionized? What about in ICP-AES? Explain.

In AA, yes it does matter. The electronic structure of an ionized metal is not the same as that of the neutral metal since one or more electrons have been removed. This changes the possible transitions and thus, the wavelengths of light that can be absorbed. Since ICP-AES is an emission technique, it does not matter

10. Is a HCL the same thing as a laser? Compare and contrast the two.

No, they are not the same. A laser begins with emission, but that emission is multiplied by a series of internal reflections (see Exhibit D). A hollow cathode lamp does not employ any methods of signal multiplication, nor are the emissions obtained from a metastable state. There is no radiationless transition involved in the decay from the excited state generated in the HCL.

11. Using the Boltzmann distribution, explain why Stokes lines are always more intense in a Raman spectrum than the anti-Stokes lines.

Actually, no calculations per se are required. Note that in the Boltzmann distribution equation (equation 5.9), the ratio of molecules in the excited state is a function of the energy gap. Assuming the degeneracy and temperatures are also constant, the relationship can be summarized as: Ratio $\approx e^{-\Delta E}$. The larger the value of ΔE, the more negative the exponent and the smaller the ratio. As illustrated in Figure 5.37, the energy gap for anti-Stokes transition is larger than that of the Stokes transition and so the ratio will always be smaller for anti-Stokes lines compared with Stokes lines.

12. A large N value is not the sole criterion for selection of a GC column for a given separation. What other factors must be taken into account?

Practical considerations such as column length, which peak the N applies to, the rate of flow needed, temperature limitations, and most importantly, the polarity and selectivity of the stationary phase must be considered. A value of N=10,000,000 is useless if the column will not separate the analytes of interest.

13. Which of the three contributing factors to band broadening in chromatography is independent of the flow rate? Explain why.

It is the eddy diffusion/variable path factor. Think of the column as a river with stones around which the water flows. The fact that some go to the left and some to the right will not change with flow; in other words if 10% go to the left and 90% to the right, that will be the proportion regardless of how many cubic feet of water are flowing per minute.

Integrative

1. Suppose a sample of urine contains quinine, a molecule that can be excited by UV light and fluoresces strongly. How would the design of a simple colorimeter/spectrometer have to be modified to detect the fluorescence and not the transmitted light coming from the excitation source?

Since the visible light from the source will travel in essentially a straight line, it makes no sense to put the detector in a straight line from the source since both the absorption/transmission and fluorescence signals will be superimposed. Since fluorescence will be in all directions, the detector should be placed at an angle off of the straight line. This is what is done in actual practice.

2. The development of the technology for micro-Raman methods has been much more difficult than for traditional IR methods. What factors contribute to this difficulty?

It is primarily the weak signal. Scattering interactions are far weaker than absorption and so detectors have to be very sensitive and sources very intense. This is in direct conflict with the fundamentals of microscopy in which low intensity and signals are of interest.

3. The light from a hollow cathode lamp is intense at discrete wavelengths, but it is not necessarily monochromatic. Explain. Is this an advantage, disadvantage, or neither?

An HCL is specific to an element because that element is used to construct it. Any allowable electronic transitions associated with that element can occur in the lamp just as they can occur in the free metal in the flame. This can be an advantage under some circumstances such as when the primary absorbance of interest is shared by more than one component in the matrix. If so, at least there are other wavelengths emitted by the lamp that could be used.

4. In the case of the assassination of President John F. Kennedy, a key piece of forensic evidence was provided by the analysis of bullets and fragments recovered. Research this case, describe how the elemental analysis was done, and discuss some of the limitations of the instrumental technique used. How would such an analysis be accomplished today?

The results are summarized in *Food for thought*, question 2b. A reasonable alternative would be ICP-OES with multiple elements. However, see *Food for thought* question 2C for additional considerations.

5. Use the concepts of scattering and polarizability to draw links between atomic and molecular scattering, refractive index, and Raman spectroscopy.

First, look at the figure presented in Exhibit B depicting how refraction occurs based on chemical structure and molecular interactions. A light wave is an oscillating electromagnetic wave that interacts with electron clouds in a crystal. Similarly, in Raman spectroscopy, (Figure 5.36), an oscillating beam of light is generating oscillations in a bond. The greater that polarization, the greater the signal; similarly, the greater the interaction of the light with a crystal, the greater the refraction.

6. Calibration of spectroscopic methods is based on Beer's Law and the linear relationship of the form y = mx + b. Theoretically, b should be zero but usually it is not. Why?

This is because we cannot create a curve that is close enough to a zero concentration to be sure that extrapolation backwards will take the curve through the origin. For example, assume that the LOQ of a given instrument and analyte is 1.0 ppm, a small concentration but still infinitely larger than zero. A ppb is 1000 times smaller, but not detectable in this hypothetical situation and so extrapolating this particular curve back from the LOQ is assuming that the curve remains linear over three orders of magnitude. Keep in mind that many instruments today are capable of detecting materials in the parts-per-trillion range and below, so extrapolating over six orders of magnitude (a factor of a million) would be involved.

7. Most manufacturers send with new GC columns test runs of 5–10 peaks and calculate the number of theoretical plates for each peak rather than just for the first one. Why?

This is because peaks will broaden due to natural diffusion the longer the analyte remains in the column and the later it elutes. As per equation 5.11, the value of N is calculated based on retention time and peak width, so both factors have to be accounted for; the value of N for an early eluting peak will not be the same as N for a late eluting peak.

8. One way to dramatically increase the sensitivity of a quadrupole mass spectrometer is to use a technique called selected ion monitoring (SIM). Explain how this technique works and why it improves sensitivity. Forensically, why is SIM rarely used? Is there a compromise between a large mass range scan and SIM? Explain.

SIM works by setting the quadrupole electrons to collect data for one ion rather than for the entire range of ions. Since no scanning steps are involved, the signal for the selected ion is much stronger; the detector does not waste time collecting signal from any other ion. The disadvantage of the technique is that no mass spectrum is collected, so the ability to identify compounds is lost.

9. Discuss and explain why the intensity of the source in any type of spectroscopy fundamentally controls the instrument's LOD and LOQ. Why does interferometry change this?

Think of signal intensity as that which you have to work with. The figure summarizes the problem: In all cases, the sample absorbs 10 units of intensity. In case A, the original intensity of the source is 100 units and the

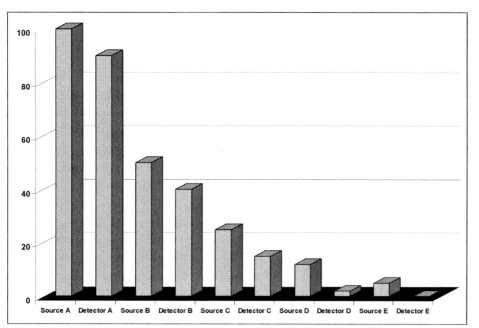

signal reaching the detector is still strong at 90 units. However, as the source intensity decreases, the relative proportion of that signal depleted by that same sample increases. In cases D and E, source intensity of 15 and 5, even a small absorbance of 10 units depletes the original signal to the point that it cannot be detected and/or quantitated.

10. There is a form of MS that utilizes the Fourier transform. Research this technique; explain how it works, how it is used, and what the advantages and disadvantages are. Is there any incentive for forensic labs to adopt FTMS over existing quadrupole designs?

FTMS is extraordinarily powerful in terms of mass resolution and in the mass range that it can address. It is also complex; the figure presents a is a greatly simplified version.

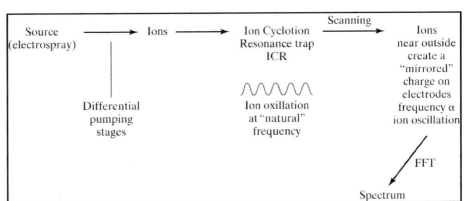

Ions are created via electrospray and are introduced into a chamber called the ICR chamber, which acts as a filter and a detector. Any ion that exists in a magnetic field will oscillate at a frequency that depends on its mass. Scanning is accomplished by directing a pulse of RF energy into the chamber at a set frequency. This change in the environment causes ions to move into stable orbits that will depend on the ion's m/z ratio and the applied radiofrequency. Ions that orbit at the periphery of the trap will induce a charge on the metal walls of that chamber and since ions are moving in a circular path and oscillating at their particular natural frequency, a mirror image of that oscillation is created on the walls of the container. The walls are in fact electrodes that will record the oscillation that characterizes the ion. As the applied Rf is changed, different ions move to the periphery. Since the ions are in a trap, this process can be repeated just as in FTIR. While FTMS is powerful, it is overkill for typical forensic needs; however, it could be useful for research related to toxicology and isotope ratios. A good summary article for this technique is: Marshall, A.G. "Milestones in Fourier transform ion cyclotron resonance mass spectrometry technique development." *International Journal of Mass Spectrometry*, 200(103), **2000**, p. 331–356.

11. Spectroscopy in the UV/VIS range produces broad bands for reasons discussed above. In addition, rotational and vibrational modes contribute to band broadening even though these quantum states and transitions are not targeted. Explain. Would performing the analysis in the gas phase alter this? Forensically, would any additional information be gained?

Rotational and vibrational modes are superimposed on any interactions that occur at higher energies. For example, refer to Figure 5.25. This diagram illustrates how one major transition (the large energy gap) in reality involves sublevels at each of the major energy levels. Performing the analysis in the gas phase would reduce band broadening by reducing interactions between solvents and neighbors, but it will not change the vibrational and rotational broadening to any significant degree.

Food for thought

1. Although it is easy to use, there are difficulties associated with the Michel-Levy chart and its applications. What might those be? In what other areas could this be an issue in forensic analysis?

The chart depends on the user's ability to interpret and match colors. Since each person has different abilities, the individual nature of color perception could lead to difficulties. This would be true whenever color was an issue (at least objectively) such as in the description of inks, paints, and textile colors.

2.

a) For the elemental analysis of bullets, what would be "better," a surface analysis technique such as XRF or a bulk analysis such as ICP-AES? Explore each technique and discuss the pros and cons of each.

A surface analysis, even using several locations, by definition never looks at the totality of the composition. If the bullet's composition is homogenous for all elements of interest, surface analysis would be acceptable, but it does require that this assumption be made. A bulk analysis would be a better choice, in general.

b) Research how the bullets involved in the assassination of John F. Kennedy were analyzed and critique the procedures and results.

The analysis was performed using neutron activation, a sensitive surface technique that requires a nuclear reactor. Elemental identification and quantitation are provided by this technique, which was done in 1963 and repeated in 1977. The results were compelling, particularly as related to the "magic bullet." A reasonable critique would be related to the surface versus bulk analysis issue. A summary of the work done in 1977 is found in: Guinn, V.P. "JFK Assassination: Bullet Analyses." *Analytical Chemistry* 51(4), **1979**, p. 484A.

c) A recent report, commissioned by the FBI and published by the National Research Council, discusses the use of elemental analysis and "chaining" as a method of analysis and interpretation of the composition of bullets. Find this report, read it, and describe what chaining is and how it is used. Critique the method and offer alternatives, keeping in mind the typical forensic lab capabilities and time pressures.

The method used to analyze the bullets in this case was ICP-OES and seven elements were targeted: As, Sb, Sn, Cu, Bi, Ag, and Cd. The Academy agreed that the analytical method was reasonable and appropriate; however, they took issue with the analysis and interpretation of the data via a technique called "chaining:"

...compares each evidence bullet (both from the crime scene and from the suspect, and which cannot be eliminated based on physical comparison) to the next sequentially to identify compositional groups in which all bullets and fragments are analytically indistinguishable within 2 standard deviations of each element's average concentration. The standard deviation (SD) of each elemental concentration is determined on the basis of the variation found among all bullets and fragments analyzed for the particular case under investigation. If all seven of the concentration intervals (from mean − 2SD to mean + 2SD) of any of the crimescene fragments fall within one of the compositional groups formed by the suspect's bullets, the fragments and matching suspect's bullets are stated to be "analytically indistinguishable."

This quote comes from the executive summary of the report. In effect, any overlap between questioned and known in the 2 SD range is considered to be indistinguishable. The Academy took issue with this and recommended that a statistical hypothesis test be used, such as the t-test of means to which a probability can be assigned.

The report was also critical of the failure to take into account the method of manufacturing and distribution of the bullets as a factor in data interpretation as noted in the following quote: *"Finding: Variations among and within lead bullet manufacturers make any modeling of the general manufacturing process unreliable and potentially misleading in CABL comparisons."* (CABL = chemical analysis of bullet lead)

Note: The report is available online from the NRC and can be read for no charge at this site: http://www.nap.edu/books/0309090792/html (current as of mid-2005); if this link is no longer active, search the National Academy Press website (www.nap.edu) using the key words "bullet analysis"

As for alternatives, the issues here are not so much analytical as statistical; bullet lead comparisons could still be done using ICP-OES as long as a defensible comparison test was used and the results were properly interpreted and reported. The term "analytically indistinguishable" may be true in the chemical sense, but when presented in this terminology and without the appropriate background and qualifiers, it is easy to see how a trier-of-fact could misinterpret this statement.

3. Does a HPLC-PDA instrument provide the same level of qualitative and quantitative information as a GCMS?

No, although the PDA provides a complete UV/VIS spectrum at each interval in the spectrum just as a mass spectrometer provides a mass spectrum at each point in the chromatogram, a UV/VIS spectrum does not provide definitive identification of the compound.

An Overview of Drugs and Pharmacology	CHAPTER 6

From the chapter

1. Why is it increasingly difficult to classify drugs as natural, semi-synthetic, or synthetic?

This is because so many drugs that were once extracted from natural products or derived from these extracts can now be made synthetically without using "natural" plant or animal extracts.

2. From a regulatory and analytical perspective, why would immediate precursors be of more concern than distant precursors?

The more steps that are needed to convert a precursor to a drug, the less likely a clandestine chemist is to use these materials. Each conversion involves loss of product, time, and money.

3. For over-the-counter preparations, inactive ingredients are called fillers. Are these the equivalent of diluents, adulterants, impurities, contaminants, or thinners? Why or why not?

Diluents and thinners as defined in this text are inactive ingredients and would be analogous to fillers. Adulterants are active and thus, are not analogous. Impurities and contaminants may or may not be active, be they in clandestine or commercially prepared materials.

4. How is the process of fractionation similar to partitioning?

Fractionation is, in effect, partitioning based on mass. The separation process is based on differences in physical properties rather than chemical, but is still based on a relative affinity. For example, water with ^{18}O rather than ^{16}O is heavier and will have a greater affinity for the liquid phase over the solid phase.

5. How would the presence of sugar as a diluent affect isotope ratio determinations of a heroin or cocaine sample? What does this imply for sample preparation for such determinations?

Since sugar is derived from a plant, the impact could be significant if there is no pre-separation of these components. The sugar used to dilute a drug sample may not have been added at the source and including it in isotope ratio determinations will only confuse the situation.

6 What practical reasons could explain the fact that oxygen and hydrogen ratios are not as commonly used to profile plant-derived drugs compared with nitrogen and carbon ratios?

These masses are well into the lower mass ranges in which interference from air can be significant.

7. Could isotope ratios be used to determine if a heroin or cocaine sample was synthesized versus extracted from a plant? Justify.

It is possible; a plant-derived material would be expected to show ppm values within some range associated with plants, even if that range is relatively large. Since a truly synthetic compound would be made independent of any plant products or derivatives, the ratios could conceivably fall far outside the expected range of plant extracts.

8. Would a profile based on residual solvents be useful for geographic location of origin? Why or why not?

No, it is not useful because there is no way to know the origin of the solvents. The isotope ratios in plants are dependent on where they are grown, whereas the isotope ratios in solvents are a function of a myriad of unpredictable factors.

9. Based on material presented in this chapter, what would be the expected metabolic elimination pathway for isopropyl alcohol?

The pathway would be expected to be similar to that of ethanol as shown in Figure 6.23. Isopropyl is not much larger than ethanol and so absorption through small pores in the stomach would seem likely. Distribution would be rapid due to the water solubility of isopropanol. About 10% would be eliminated unchanged, while the remaining 90% would be subject to dehydrogenation to acetone rather than the aldehyde given that the –OH group is on an interior carbon and not an end carbon. Acetone is water soluble and could be eliminated as is, or there could be further metabolism in the liver; however, based on the material presented in the text, this is as far as we can go.

10. Why is it more effective to administer morphine by injection rather than by oral ingestion?

So much of morphine is lost during first pass metabolism. As a result, an oral dose must be much higher than an injected dose to obtain the same therapeutic concentration in the plasma.

11. A woman weighing 60 kg drinks the equivalent of 60 g of ethanol. Her peak plasma concentration was found to be 1.91 g/L.

   a) What is the value of V_d for ethanol in this example?

$$V_d = \frac{D}{C_p \, Kg} = \frac{60g}{1.91\frac{g}{L} \; 60kg} = 0.52\frac{L}{kg}$$

   b) Assume that the woman's weight is 55% water. How does the weight of water in her body and the V_d value compare? What does this mean in terms of the distribution of ethanol?

55% of 60 kg = 33 kg of water. Assuming a density of 1, this is 33 liters of water. The volume of distribution of this dose is 33L/60kg or 0.55 L kg^{-1}. This indicates that ethanol is water soluble and that anywhere there is water in the body, ingested ethanol will find its way there.

12. The predator drug Rohypnol (flunitrazepam) when administered orally has a bioavailability (F) of 70%. A woman arrives unconscious in the emergency room with signs that a sexual assault may have occurred within the last hour. She weighs 120 lbs and a blood analysis reveals a C_p of this compound of 0.50 mg/L. Estimate the size of the initial dose in mg, assuming this is the peak concentration. Is it conceivable that a dose of this size could be administered surreptitiously in an alcoholic beverage?

First, convert the body weight of 120 lbs to 54.5 kg. According to Clarke's Handbook, the V_d of this drug (p. 1045, Volume 2), is between 3.5 and 5.5 L kg^{-1}, so we'll use the middle value of 4.5 L kg^{-1}. Rearrange equation 6.8 to obtain:

$D = V_d * C_p * kg = 4.5$ L kg^{-1} $* 0.50$ mg L^{-1} $* 54.4$ kg or 122.4 mg.

This represents 70% of the original dose, so correct it upwards by dividing 122/.70 to yield 175 mg. Such a small dose could be added to a drink without detection.

13. According to the CRC Handbook of Chemistry and Physics (84th edition), the accepted natural isotopic abundance of ^{13}C is cited as 1.07% of all carbon. What would be the δ % value of a 1.00 g sample of carbon that had this isotopic ratio?

It would have to be the same. In terms of ppm, a value of 1.07% can be converted to 1.07 part-per-hundred, 10.7 parts-per-thousand, and 10,700 parts per million.

Integrative

1. Photosynthesis is the key partitioning process for fractionation of carbon in plants. Illustrate this process and determine which isotope of carbon would be preferentially fractionated by this fixation.

To greatly simplify, the process of photosynthesis can be summarized as the conversion of atmospheric CO_2 and H_2O to O_2 and glucose, which is in turn converted to starch and cellulose. This occurs within the structure of the plant, so it would be expected that the heavier carbon isotope 13C would be slightly enriched in the plant relative to the atmosphere around it.

2. Given the following data regarding aspirin:

pKa	$t_{1/2}$ plasma	Principal metabolic reaction	Conjugates with	~LD_{50}
3.5	17 minutes	hydrolysis	Glucuronic acid	225 mg/kg

Source: Galichet, L. Y., et al., ed., "Aspirin," *Clarke's Analysis of Drugs and Poisons.*

London: Pharmaceutical Press, 2004, p. 652.

Answer the following questions:

a) What is the lethal dose for an adult female (130 lbs) reported in number of tablets of aspirin, which typically contain 325 mg of aspirin?

$$LD \approx 59.0 kg \frac{225 mg}{kg} = \frac{13268 mg}{325 \frac{mg}{tab}} \approx 41 \, tablets$$

b) Can the plasma half-life be used to determine how long aspirin will remain in the tissues? Explain.

No, as plasma concentration decreases, this can correspond to an increase of concentration in other compartments. It does not always correlate directly to elimination from the body. All we know is that it is out of the plasma; we do not necessarily know where it went.

c) Assuming a first-order process and rapid absorption, what would be the concentration of aspirin in the woman an hour after she took two 325 mg tablets?

We will work with the first order decay relationships eq. 6.5–6.7. The half-life is used to determine the needed rate constant:

$k = 0.693/17 \, min = 0.041 min^{-1}$

Next we will need to determine what the peak plasma concentration is since we will assume this is the C_0 in the decay equation. This is achieved using the volume of distribution:

$$C_p = \frac{D}{V_d \, kg} = \frac{650 mg}{0.15 \frac{L}{kg} 59.0 kg} = 73.4 \frac{mg}{L} = C_0$$

Now use the decay expression to obtain C_t:

$lnC_t = -0.041 min^{-1} * 120 min + ln(73.4)$

$lnC_t = -0.62$

$C_t = 0.54 \, mg \, L^{-1}$

d) Show the hydrolysis of aspirin and the expected product.

e) At what stage (ADME) does conjugation play a role?

Conjugation occurs in the plasma and can continue into the urine.

f) Where is aspirin absorbed preferentially in the GI tract? Justify with calculations.

This is where it is neutral, at pH of 1.5 or less, which would be found in the stomach.

3. The following data applies to the drug Rohypnol (flunitrazepam), FW 313.3:

Log P	pK$_a$	Structure	t$_{1/2}$ plasma	t$_{1/2}$ elimination	Elimination	Color test
2.1	1.8		3 h	16–35 h	1% unchanged urine; 10% feces and the rest metabolites in urine	Marquis: Orange

Source: Galichet, L. Y., et al., ed., *Clarke's Analysis of Drugs and Poisons - Volume 2*. London: Pharmaceutical Press, 2004.

Answer the following questions:

a) Where in the gastrointestinal tract is flunitrazepam absorbed preferentially? Justify with calculations.

Absorption is generally favored when the drug is in the neutral stage. Since this drug is basic with a pKa of 1.8, then any pH exceeding ~4 will insure that the concentration of the drug in the neutral state >>> concentration in the ionized state. Such calculations were conducted in Chapter 4.

b) Assuming a typical dose of 1 mg, what would be the expected concentration of unchanged drug in a urine sample of 25 ml?

10% of this, or 0.1mg, would be unchanged, but this is a simplistic assumption that ignores time factors. This assumption is necessary given how the question is worded.

c) If the LOD/LOQ for this drug in a mass spectrometer is 2.5 ug/L, how long after the dose will it be possible to detect the unmetabolized drug in urine?

Since the LOD is 2.5 ug/L in a volume of 25 mL, this corresponds 2.5 ug/L * 0.025L = 0.063 ug total in the urine sample. This is the amount excreted, which in turn represents 10% of the original dosage, or 0.63 mg, in the urine. Now we can apply the first-order decay expression using C_t as 0.63 as the concentration at time t and solve for that time. To obtain the value of the rate constant, use equation 6.5:

$$k = \frac{0.693}{26 \text{ hours}} = 0.027 \, hr^{-1}$$

Also realize that we can use C_0 as 1 mg and the natural log of 1 is zero and so the final expression, based on rearranging equation 6.7 is:

$$\ln(0.63) = -0.027 hr^{-1} t \text{ and } t \approx 17 \text{ hours.}$$

Note that the half-life of 26 hours was selected as the middle of the range provided. The dose can be treated as a weight because although we do not have an example body weight, for any given person, the volume will be constant. For this type of approximation, this is a reasonable step.

d) Propose a sample extraction scheme for this substance from blood.

While it might be possible to extract using a LLE method, the matrix of blood is not well-suited to this approach. Better would be an extraction with a solid phase capable of binding the neutral drug such as C18 (octadecyl). The sample would be made basic enough to suppress ionization, with a pH ~6 introduced into the column. After rinsing and washing, an acidic media could be used to flush the ionized base out. Note this is one of many possible extraction schemes.

e) The three major peaks in the mass spectrum of this drug are 312, 285, 266, and 238. Propose fragment losses to explain.

The fragments can be rationalized as losses from the M-H peak at 312 as well as from 313. The 285 peak is a loss of 27 amu, typical of a methyl group (15) and a CH (17), which could come from breakage of the ring structure. The loss of 46 could represent the loss of the NO_2

from the M-H structure. Finally, the fragment at 238 likely represents the loss of one benzene ring C_6H_3 from within the linked ring structure.

f) Based on the structure of the drug, what distinctive IR spectra features might be expected?

For a drug molecule, the fluorine and NO_2 groups attached to phenyl rings will be distinctive. Refer to the Appendix with the IR information and note that these features are expected to produce strong bands in the range of ~1300–1000cm^{-1} for the C-F feature and ~1600, 1400, and 600cm^{-1} for the R-NO_2 group.

4. Find out the chemical structure for mescaline. This is a potent hallucinogen that is derived from the peyote cactus and is one of the oldest known hallucinogens. Is this hallucinogen a tryptamine or a phenethylamine?

Mescaline has a single ring structure and as such is a phenethylamine.

5. Using Table 6.3 and a statistical/scientific graphing program, create a 3-D scatterplot of the data as might be prepared for court. Prepare a second such plot that incorporates error bars. Comment on their importance.

Without uncertainties:

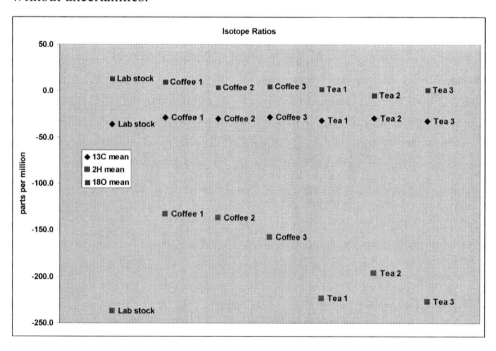

With uncertainties:

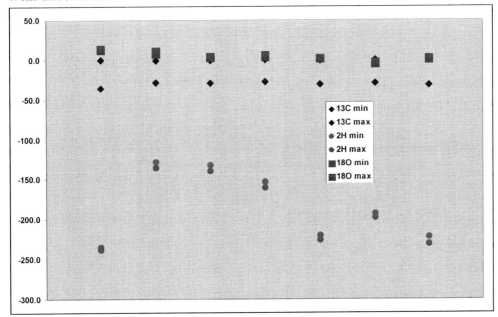

When uncertainties are included, what might appear to be different values for the ppm begin to overlap; at the least, a t-test of means would be needed to sort out what differences are significant and which are not. As one example, look at the data in the first plot for 2H; note that what appears to be a difference among the three coffees changes significantly with the uncertainty included.

Food for thought

1. Is caffeine an addictive substance? If so, is it psychologically addictive, physiologically addictive, or both? What about chocolate? Bubble gum? How are such distinctions made?

Yes, coffee is psychologically and physiologically addictive. The latter is due to the appearance of withdrawal symptoms such as the "caffeine headache" and the tolerance people can develop toward this drug. In light of the lack of physical symptoms, chocolate and bubble gum would not be considered physiologically addictive, but certainly for many people, these substances are psychologically addictive.

Forensic Drug Analysis I

From the chapter

1. Summarize the mechanisms by which color can be created using a color test reagent.

-dye formation

-condensation and coupling

-transition metal complexes

-redox

2. Why are reagents based on formation of diazonium ions and salts used almost exclusively for alkaloids and bases?

The diazonium ions are formed by the reaction of amines and nitrous acid, and basic drugs (alkaloids) are amines. Also, in coupling reactions, the diazonium ion is a weak electrophile that can react with activated ring compounds. One way to activate a ring is to incorporate an amine substituent on in.

3. What would happen if the Liebermann reagent was added to a sample of cocaine HCl? Why? Give a defensible chemical explanation.

Cocaine does not have a phenolic group, but it is an alkaloid so a color change is expected.

4. The nitroprusside reaction will not work (i.e., not produce colored products) with primary and secondary amines if the pH is acidic. Why?

Under acidic conditions, the basic drug will exist in the $BH+$ form, which will not react with the reagent.

5. Related to the previous question, why would NaOH be a poor choice for the base as opposed to sodium carbonate?

NaOH is a strong base and the –OH can participate in undesired side reactions.

6. In reference 17, the following statement is made: "…when a chloroform solution of indole is treated with dilute acid (up to approximately 12 percent) and Ehrlich's reagent the color remains in the chloroform, but if the test is made with stronger hydrochloric acid the color is transferred to the aqueous phase. If the acid is too concentrated, the color may be inhibited or destroyed." Offer an explanation.

Moving from the chloroform to the aqueous layer indicates that the species has somehow acquired a charge, probably as a result of protonation at an amine site. Additional acid must be causing degradation or decoupling; some reaction is disrupting the conjugated system.

7. Name the functional group(s) in THC. What presumptive color/crystal tests could be useful aside from the Duquenois-Levine test? Why are crystal tests of limited use with plant extracts?

Phenol is the predominant functionality and so a Liebermann or ferric chloride test might be appropriate. Plants are complex mixtures and mixtures are not well-suited for crystal tests.

8. Resorcinol gives a false positive with the Duquenois-Levine test. Why?

Resorcinol is a phenyl di-alcohol and would be expected to behave somewhat like THC, which is a phenolic compound as well.

9. One test occasionally performed on aqueous solutions containing a mixture of GHB and GBL is to test for elevated concentrations of K^+ or Na^+. Why?

A common method of manufacturing GHB clandestinely is to combine GBL with a base such as NaOH or KOH. Finding these ions at elevated concentrations is suggestive of this route.

10. Give the specific mechanism of the conversion of GHB to GBL. Would a mix of products be expected?

A mixture is not expected; there are no opportunities for alternative products as shown.

11. Name a presumptive test or test series that could distinguish between testosterone and estradiol and justify the selection.

The key difference between the two compounds is the phenyl alcohol group found on estradiol and not on the testosterone. Liebermann's test targets phenols and would be useful. Note in Clarke's, this reagent turns black, which is a confirmation of this selection.

12. Explain what is meant by the term "undetectable" when referring to a designer steroid. Obviously it is a misnomer if taken literally since such compounds have been identified.

This term implies that the substance or its metabolic products cannot be detected by current methods either due to their chemical natural or to low concentrations.

13. The following colors are obtained in presumptive testing:

Steroid	Liebermann's	Mandelin's
Testosterone	Light violet	Orange-red
Testosterone cypionate	Orange-brown	Dark brown
Testosterone enanthate	No reaction	Orange-red
Testosterone propionate	Orange-brown	Orange-brown

Explain/justify these observations. Source: Chiong, D. M., et al. "The Analysis and Identification of Steroids." *Journal of Forensic Sciences,* **37 1992, 488–502.**

To explain the results, turn to the structures of the molecules (Table 7.7) and combine this with specificity of the color tests listed. The core structure of linked rings is the same in all; differences are seen in the attachments to the rightmost 5-carbon ring as drawn in the table. Any differences in the results would be attributed to differences in these attached groups.

Liebermann's reagent targets phenols and amines, the latter of which is not an issue here. The light violet is interesting, but not easily rationalized; however, the orange-brown colors were reported for those compounds with carbonyl functionalities. The Mandelin reagent contains vanadium and forms colored transition metal complexes with Lewis bases such as oxygen and so strong positive results are not surprising here.

Integrative

1. Calculate the minimum and maximum frequencies and energies of a photon capable of promoting an electron with UV/VIS radiation.

Maximum energy: wavelength = 200nm; minimum energy = 700 nm; equation needed: $c = \lambda\upsilon$ with $c = 3 \times 10^8$ m sec^{-1}. Rearrange to solve for the frequency as $\upsilon = c/\lambda$. Note that wavelengths must be converted to meters:

$\upsilon_{max} = 3 \times 10^8$ m sec^{-1}/2.00×10^{-7} m $= 1.50 \times 10^{15}$ sec^{-1}

$\upsilon_{min} = 3 \times 10^8$ m sec^{-1}/7.00×10^{-7} m $= 4.29 \times 10^{14}$ sec^{-1}

2. Set up a spreadsheet and use it to determine the ratio of protonated to unprotonated cocaine at the following pH values: 1.0 (such as if concentrated HCl were used), 2.0, 4.0, 6.0 (typical of laboratory distilled water used in reagent preparation), 6.6 (pK$_a$ – 2.0), 7.0, 8.6, 9.0, 10.0, 10.6 (pK$_a$ + 2.0), and 12. Make the spreadsheet as generic as possible so other compounds and other pKa values can be substituted. Graph the results showing the concentration of the two species as a function of pH.

Cocaine is a weak base with a pKa of 8.6; use the expression given in Figure 4.7 to set up the spreadsheet using the modified equation pH – pK$_a$ = log ([B]/[BH+])

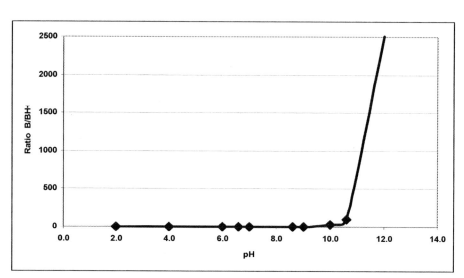

pK$_a$:	8.6	
pH	**Log Ratio**	**Ratio B/BH+**
2.0	-6.6	0
4.0	-4.6	0
6.0	-2.6	0
6.6	-2.0	0
7.0	-1.6	0
8.6	0.0	1
9.0	0.4	3
10.0	1.4	25
10.6	2.0	100
12.0	3.4	2512

Notice that the pKa value is stored in a separate cell such that this spreadsheet can be used for other drugs. Also note the expected behavior (always comforting) that the basic drug is in the neutral form in basic solutions and is more ionized in acidic solutions, which would favor the BH+ form.

Using the preceding data, information in the chapter, and supplementary information as needed (i.e., references), answer/explain the following:

For these problems, it is a good idea to summarize what you know ahead of time, as shown in the box to the right:

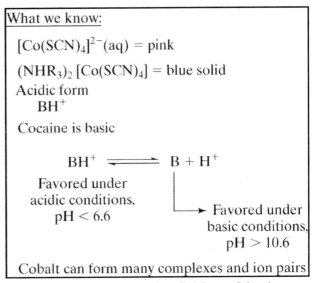

What we know:

$[Co(SCN)_4]^{2-}$ (aq) = pink

$(NHR_3)_2 [Co(SCN)_4]$ = blue solid

Acidic form
  BH^+

Cocaine is basic

$$BH^+ \rightleftharpoons B + H^+$$

Favored under acidic conditions, pH < 6.6

Favored under basic conditions, pH > 10.6

Cobalt can form many complexes and ion pairs

a) A "one well" approach is a variation of the cobalt thiocyanate test. In it, the cobalt thiocyanate reagent is dissolved in 98 mL of water to which 2 mL of con HCl is added. When the solution is first prepared, it turns blue, but there is no precipitate formed. The color eventually reverts to pink. Explain and discuss the implications for field test kits.*

* Source: Deakin, A. L. "A Study of Acids Used for the Acidified Cobalt Thiocyanate Test for Cocaine Base." *Microgram Journal,* 1 2003, 40–44.

The reference cited offers critical clues, as does part b below. This color change was observed only with concentrated HCl and not with other acids, which indicates that the transitory complex that forms contains some chloride. Since no solid is observed, this is further evidence of a transition metal complex. The kinetics of this formation are faster than that of the pink SCN- complex, which is apparently more stable. The formation of $[CoCl_4]^{2-}$, a pink complex, is favored due to a localized increase in the concentration of chloride from the HCl.

b) In an experiment similar to that described in part a, it was observed that if 0.1N HCl was used instead of con HCl, no transitory color change was observed and the test worked as expected with cocaine.

* Source: Deakin, A. L. "A Study of Acids Used for the Acidified Cobalt Thiocyanate Test for Cocaine Base." *Microgram Journal,* 1 2003, 40–44.

This adds confidence to the hypothesis; less acid means less Cl⁻.

c) Cocaine can hydrolyze in solution when exposed to strong acids or bases, but the process typically requires hours. Give equations/reactions for the hydrolysis under both conditions and state the likely products.

As with aspirin, hydrolysis affects the –OH groups and will cleave the cocaine into two molecules as shown at right:

Source: Kovar, K.A. and M. Laudszun. *Chemistry and Reaction Mechanisms of Rapid Tests for Drugs of Abuse and Precursor Chemicals.* United Nations Scientific and Technical Notes, 1989.

d) The Scott variant consists of a cobalt thiocyanate solution that is prepared in 1:1 water and glycerin. When this is added to a cocaine sample, the characteristic blue precipitate forms. The test continues by the addition of HCl until a precipitate-free pink solution is observed. The solution is extracted with chloroform. The bottom layer is blue, the top pink. Explain. What is the likely function of the glycerin? Source: Schlesinger, H. L. "Topics in the Chemistry of Cocaine." *United Nations Office on Drugs and Crime: Bulletin on Narcotics,* 1985, 63–85.

We know the identification of the blue solid; we also know that the cobalt will complex with Cl- as indicated in parts a and b. Cocaine is still present in the solution, but how it is complexing is not clear from the evidence provided. However, when chloroform is added, what transfers to the lower chloroform layer will be neutral species; so, we can hypothesize that the pink in the top layer is the cobalt-thiocyanate complex and in the lower layer is the solubilized ion-pair (which will be neutral) that contains cocaine. The function of the glycerin could be stabilization of neutral complexes or perhaps a reduction of the activity of Cl⁻.

e) What other transition metals might work as ion-pair reagents? List 2–3 and discuss the considerations and experiments that would be needed to use them.

Based on the above results cobalt, copper, molybdenum, and chromium would be reasonable choices based on availability, electron structure, known colored coordinate compounds, and toxicity. Simple experiments with common drugs such as cocaine, heroin, and methamphetamine under various pH conditions would be a reasonable first step.

3. One colored species proposed for some stable carbocation color change reactions is a tropylium ion. Why would a tropylium ion be expected to be colored or a different color than the starting material?

The tropylium cation is cycloheptatrienyl cation, which is an aromatic that has multiple resonance forms; these are fundamental to generating color.

4. Fast Blue B has been used as a spray reagent developer for TLC of marijuana samples and as a color test reagent. Due to its carcinogenic properties, the Fast Blue BB salt has replaced it in most uses. Find the formula for Fast Blue BB and postulate how it reacts with the THC, CBN, and CBD. Why are the colors developed with Fast Blue B different for the three cannabinoids? Which two would you expect to be the most similar?

Refer to Table 7.6 for the structures of interest and note differences. First, CBD is a diol ,while the other two are mono-alcohols. We can also gather clues from the colors produced. CBN-FBB is purple and so the energy gaps are smaller relative to the CBD and THC products. Now refer to Figure 7.20, which shows how the salt forms an azo dye. The core structure, the linkage between FBB and the phenyl ring is the same for all three compounds; the difference in color arises from the difference in attached structures. Given the structures, the CBN/CBD would be expected to be the most similar.

5. Describe an extraction scheme to separate testosterone and estradiol.

Refer to Figure 7.43 for structures; note the presence of a second –OH group as part of a phenyl structure not found in the testosterone. Refer to Clarke's to obtain the following data:

Estradiol: insoluble in water, 1 in 28 in ethanol, 1 in 17 acetone, 1 in 435 chloroform, 1 in 150 ether. Soluble in dioxane and alkali hydroxides.

Testosterone: not soluble in dioxane or alkali hydroxides.

Separation can be effected using either dioxane or a basic solution such as NaOH.

6. Of the compounds shown in Table 7.7, several are generally provided in solution for injection. What would the solvent likely be and why?

Water is not likely to be used since these are lipophilic molecules, so an organic solvent would be needed; however, toxicity must be considered. Ethanol is one possibility.

7. *This question has been moved to a subsequent chapter.*

Food for thought

1. A common scene in movies and TV programs shows the detective tasting a suspected drug powder to determine its identity. In addition to being poor laboratory practice, it is a really bad idea. Discuss and explain.

First, tasting a substance is a poor presumptive test; all alkaloids will taste bitter since they are bases. Second, tasting an unknown white powder in the home of a suspect would seem to be a really bad move.

2. How important is it for a forensic chemist to understand why heroin turns the Marquis reagent purple or why cocaine forms a blue precipitate with the cobalt thiocyanate reagent?

Understanding how a test works allows a chemist to interpret results, particularly when something new or unusual is observed. Understanding the chemistry behind the tests allows for reasonable hypotheses to explain such results and can lead to significant insights. However, since color tests are the first step in a detailed analysis and since identification does not hinge on results of this test alone, knowing every facet of the test would not be essential; just very useful.

Drug Analysis II: Basic Drugs

From the chapter

1. Would a sample of heroin containing significantly more 3-MAM verses 6-MAM be noteworthy? Why? What could this indicate?

Refer to Figure 8.11 and note that 3-MAM is an intermediate seen as morphine is converted to heroin, while 6-MAM is a degradation product. Finding significant amounts of 3-MAM, which is less stable than the 6-MAM, could be indicative of a fresh batch in which some incomplete conversion occurred.

2. For any given molecule of heroin, what % of the carbon originates from morphine and what percentage is traceable to acetic anhydride, assuming that is the reagent used in the conversion.

There are 17 carbons in morphine and 21 in heroin, the difference being 4 carbons, 2 from each added acetate group. By number of carbons, this corresponds to 19% of the carbon atoms coming from acetic anhydride.

3. On the basis of your answer to Problem 2, and using chemical equations and diagrams, explain how the acetylation of morphine will alter the $^{13}C/^{12}C$ ratio of a sample. From the perspective of profiling, is this alteration the source of potentially useful information or does it merely confuse the situation? Justify.

Based on the answer above, ~20% of the atoms in a given sample of pure heroin prepared by acetylation of plant-derived morphine will come from non-plant sources. The only way to tease out these contributions would be to take this into account when looking at the isotope ratios of specific fragment ions. To isolate the plant contribution, fragment ions that do not include the added acetate groups would have to be used. If this could be done, then profiling would be of value; if not, then the results will likely not be useful for sourcing.

4. One of the difficulties in profiling of plant-derived drugs is obtaining reliable standards. Elaborate.

First, someone has to go to the location, not always a simple or safe proposition. Second, even within a geographical region, variations are expected and so representative samples are needed. Third, seasonal variations are expected, as are variations within a single plant.

5. Caffeine is an alkaloid base with a bitter taste that is cheap and easy to obtain. It is frequently used as an adulterant of cocaine, but is rarely used as an adulterant of heroin. Why?

As an adulterant, caffeine is an active ingredient. Since it is a stimulant, it makes sense to use it to cut another stimulant such as cocaine. It makes less sense to use it to cut a depressant/narcotic such as heroin since the two physiological effects counteract each other.

6. What is the difference between aggregate weight and usable quantity?

An aggregate weight is the total sample weight. The usable quantity is usually defined as the amount of controlled substance present. If the aggregate weight of a cocaine exhibit is 1.0 g and the %cocaine is determined as 25%, then the usable quantity would be 0.25 g or 250 mg.

7. What is a key structural feature seen in the benzodiazepines and SSRI that is not seen in any other drugs discussed so far?

a halogen atom

8. One method used to remove the alkaloids papaverine and noscapine from extracted morphine is to scatter the powder in water and adjust the pH to 6.4. After a time, the pH is made basic (9.0) and extracted with an organic solvent. Explain how and why this works.

First, obtain solubility and pKa data from Clarke's or Merck for each of these compounds. Since they will likely be in the basic form in the plant, use that data:

Noscapine	pKa 6.2	Practically insoluble in water
Morphine	8.0 and 9.9 (amphoteric)	Soluble 1 in 5000 water
Papaverine	6.4	Soluble 1 in 40 water

Noscapine is not soluble and will stay in the powder since the pH is not acidic enough to favor the BH+ form. At a pH of 6.4, the neutral form of papaverine and the ionized form will be close to a 1:1 ratio, which will limit the extraction of the BH+ form of this compound. In contrast, the morphine will be significantly ionized at this pH. As shown in Figure 4.11, the basic group has a pKa of 8.02 and so a pH of 6.4 is relatively acidic and will favor the soluble BH+ form. A later adjustment of the pH to ~9 will favor neutral morphine at its isoelectric point, which will extract into organic solvents.

9. The following data is obtained from the PDR regarding an elixir:

TYLENOL® WITH CODEINE (Ortho-McNeil)

tablets CIII

(acetaminophen and codeine phosphate)

Contains:

>   **Codeine Phosphate** .... **12 mg**
>   **Acetaminophen** .... **120 mg**

a) Assuming that the elixir is a syrupy aqueous solution, suggest a method to isolate the two active ingredients from the syrup using SPE.

The relevant pKa values are 8.2 and 9.5, so the goal is to separate these two from the syrup matrix rather than from each other, which can be accomplished using GCMS. A solid phase such as C8 would be a reasonable choice. An aliquot of the sample would be added to a buffer with a pH of ~12 to drive both drugs to the neutral form. When introduced to the column, these forms would associate with the stationary phase. Subsequent washes with polar solvents would further clean the sample and then the solution could be eluted using acidified methanol. Note: This is an example of a reasonable approach, but not the only one that would work.

b) Make the procedure you suggested in part a quantitative for a GCMS analysis. Assume that the linear dynamic range of the curve for both drugs is 10.0–200.0 ng/mL and that the recovery of your method will be within 95–105%. Further assume an injection volume of 1.0 uL. (NOTE: There is more than one correct answer just as there are many preparations that could work. Select one that is reasonable.)

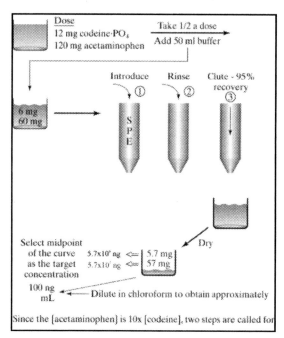

To be conservative, assume that the 95% recovery is obtained and correct accordingly. As shown in the figure, to hit the middle of the calibration curve, a separate solution of each drug will be required.

A first step would be to reconstitute the dried material in 100.0 mL of chloroform. This would yield a concentration of 5.7×10^3 ng mL^{-1} of the codeine and 5.7×10^4 ng mL^{-1} of acetaminophen since 1 mg = 10^6 ng. The next step would be dilution to the curve range and targeting 57 ng mL-1 is reasonable and makes for powers of 10 dilution. $57 = 5.7 \times 10^1$ so to get the codeine solution into the calibration range, a dilution factor of 100 (10^2) will bring the concentration down from the 10^3 range to the 10^1 range. Similarly, a 1→1000 dilution will bring acetaminophen into range. The latter could be accomplished by diluting 10 uL to 10mL for example.

c) Could this sample be extracted with an organic solvent such as chloroform and directly injected into the GCMS system as described? Why or why not?

Probably not. Chloroform will extract dyes and possibly some of the thickening agents as well, resulting in a viscous mixture. Some measure of sample preparation is preferred.

Integrative

1. Why are the functional groups attached to carbon 3 in morphine more active than those attached to carbon 6?

Carbon 3 is attached to a benzene ring, which tends to activate this carbon by electron withdrawl.

2. Suggest two alternative reagents that could be used for simple (1–2 step) conversions of lysergic acid to LSD. Show the reaction(s).

Fundamentally, the conversion task is creating a good leaving group out of a poor one, in this case –OH. Thus, similar reagents such as $POCl_3$ or thionyl chloride would fit these requirements. Indeed, these are two that are used in this role.

3. The active ingredients of khat are shown in Table 8.13. Cathinone loses its potency quickly once the plant is harvested; cathine does not. Provide a defensible chemical explanation for this.

The only structural difference is the carbonyl group; ketones can undergo hydrolysis reactions, which could explain the loss of potency.

4. Postulate a mechanism and explanation for the formation of the aziridines during the Emde method of methamphetamine synthesis.

An aziridine would result from a reaction within the molecule. In the Emde method, the –OH is converted to a –Cl group that is two carbons away from a nitrogen group. The nitrogen can attack the C-Cl to form a relatively unstable 3-membered ring.

5. Research and briefly explain how dopamine and serotonin work. Using structures presented in this chapter, postulate how and why these substances produce their characteristic effects.

Serotonin and dopamine are classified as biogenic amines and are active in the central nervous system. Serotonin performs mostly as an inhibitor, but dopamine can be inhibiting or excitatory depending on the situation.

Dopamine	Serotonin

Both of these compounds play a role in drug action and drug abuse. Stimulants such as amphetamines increase the release of dopamine, while cocaine blocks its re-uptake. The SSRI class of drugs reduces the re-uptake of serotonin and, as a result, can relieve symptoms such as anxiety and poor sleeping. Interestingly, LSD inhibits serotonin. Note that dopamine has a phenylethylamine skeleton and serotonin has structural features in common with hallucinogens described in the previous chapter.

Source: Marieb, E. N. *Human Anatomy and Physiology* 6ᵗʰ ed. San Francisco: Pearson/Benjamin Cummings, 2004. Chapter 11: Fundamentals of the Nervous System and Nervous Tissue.

6. What by-products would you expect if the Birch method is used to prepare methamphetamine from ephedrine?

Refer to Figure 8.35 for key steps; the only possibility that seems credible is for a "real" Birch reduction to occur in which the benzene ring is further reduced as per Figure 8.34. The product would look like methamphetamine except the ring would have two double bonds rather than three. This compound, 1-(1',4'-cyclohexadienyl)-2-methylaminopropane, would result. Recent work has shown that this compound is indeed produced by the Birch method.

Source: Person, E.C., Meyer, J.A., VyVyan, J.R. "Structural Determination of the Principal Byproduct of the Lithium-Ammonia Reduction Method of Methamphetamine Manufacture." *Journal of Forensic Science*, **2005**, Vol 50(1), p. 87–95.

7. One sign that the Birch/Nazi method has been used to synthesize methamphetamine is an empty propane tank like those used for barbeque grills. Such tanks have a blue patina around the valve. What could account for this?

These tanks are often used to hold anhydrous ammonia and the blue color is the result of a copper-ammonia complex.

8. Based on the fundamental characteristics of abused substances, what are some reasons for the relatively limited abuse of modern anti-anxiety and anti-depressant drugs relative to those they have replaced?

The SSRIs do not produce as many side effects as do barbiturates such as sedation and sleeping pills. When these effects do occur, they are generally less intense and will fade over time. Thus, there is little incentive for abusers to take these drugs to produce such effects.

9. This question was presented in Chapter 2 (question 9). Compare the approach that is possible now using presumptive tests and screening tests compared with the initial response and comment on the role these tests play in sample selection.

  a) A small seizure of suspected LSD is submitted to the lab and consists of 30 blotter papers. Design a sampling plan assuming that the contents of a minimum of three papers will be needed to obtain sufficient sample for presumptive and confirmatory testing.

Initially, set aside half of the exhibits and focus on the remaining 15. The first step would be to look at these 15 under UV light to see if they fluoresce. If so, this is indicative of LSD. Those that fluoresced would be selected for additional testing. Of those, half would be tested with Erlich's reagent, which will produce a purple color in the presence of LSD.

  b) After selecting and testing, all are negative. Describe the next steps in the analysis.

If negative, the remaining blotter papers that fluoresced would be tested with Erlich's.

  c) At what point in this LSD analysis would it be appropriate to call the results negative for LSD?

If all tested in part b were negative under both UV and color testing protocols.

d) Assume that all are negative until four squares are left. Testing one gives a positive result. Using a flow chart, describe the next step(s) and any assumptions made.

First, a call to the submitting agency and others as needed would be appropriate since further testing will destroy the sample. If approval is granted, an attempt could be made to extract the LSD from the blotter paper and to obtain an IR spectrum. TLC of the extract against LSD standards would also be appropriate.

Food for thought

1. If designating precursors, such as P2P as controlled substances or listed chemicals, has been successful in eliminating the method of synthesis, why not add ephedrine to Schedule I of the Controlled Substances Act?

There is movement to do so in several states and at press time, there were bills pending in Congress to limit access to the precursors. The issue that differentiates this situation from that of P2P is the widespread legitimate uses of the precursors in antihistamines and until substitutes are available, it is unlikely that pseudoephedrine and related compounds will be controlled.

The Chemistry of Combustion and Arson	CHAPTER 9

Note: Since many of these calculations are based on modeling and approximation, the significant figure rules have not been strictly applied; the key word here being "approximation."

From the chapter

1. Assume that 1.00 gram of nitroglycerin is used in a firearm as a propellant. Also assume that the combustion is 100% efficient and that 65% of the chemical energy is transferred to a bullet that weighs 115 grains. How fast will the bullet be moving? Will it exceed the speed of sound?

The approach here will be to first determine the energy released (Q) by calculating $\Delta H°$ for the reaction. Then all that is needed is to use the formula:

$$V = \sqrt{\frac{2m_pQ\eta}{m_b}}$$

in which the heat of the reaction is Q. This is a unit conversion problem since everything must cancel to leave a velocity unit such as meters/second. An online converter makes short work of these conversions, but first the heat of reaction based on the balanced equation:

$$2C_3H_5N_3O_9 \rightarrow 6CO_2 + 5H_2O + 3N_2 \text{ plus excess } O_2; \text{ assume all in the gas phase}$$

Note that O_2, while a participant in the reaction, can be omitted since it will not contribute to the calculation of the heat of reaction. Similarly, nitrogen will not contribute to the calculation of heat evolved. Fractions could have been used as well. Calculating Q (heat of reaction) can be done the hard way, by determining which bonds are broken and which are formed and calculating the net energy release. It is easier to find the standard heats of formation using the CRC or a similar reference. The values used here were obtained from the CRC, 84th edition.

$\Delta H°_{rxn} = \Sigma[\Delta H°]_{products} - \Sigma[\Delta H°]_{reactants}$ with the value of $N_2 = O_2 = 0.0 \text{kJ mol}^{-1}$.

$\Delta H°_{rxn} = [6(-393.5) + 5(-241.82)] - 2[-370.9]$ with all units in kJ mol^{-1} = -2828

This value is for 2 moles of nitroglycerin (NG), so that will have to be taken into account, leaving a value of Q = 1414 kJ/mole of NG. Now relate this value to the number of moles:

Moles of NG = 1.00g / 227g mol^{-1} = 4.41x10^{-3} moles of NG x 1414 kJ mol^{-1} = 6.2 kJ

Thus, we have already addressed the m$_p$Q term in the above equation. Now:

$$V = \sqrt{\frac{2*6.2\,kJ*0.65}{115\,grains}}$$

Units now must be converted to leave a velocity in m/s:

1 J = 1 kg m^2 s^{-2}, so convert the 6.2 kJ to 6200J;

1 grain = 0.0647989 gram, so 115 grains = 7.45 gram or 0.00745 kg:

$$V = \sqrt{\frac{2*6200\,kg\,m^2 s^{-2}*0.65}{0.00745\,kg}} \approx 1040\ m\ s^{-1}$$

This velocity exceeds the speed of sound, which is ~331 m s^{-1}.

2. How is a shotgun like a pipe bomb in terms of energy conversion? How is it different?

It is similar in that the work done is transferred to several small pieces of metal rather than to one large projectile as in a pistol or a rifle. The shotgun is designed to send all of the projectiles in one general direction rather than in all directions as in the case of a pipe bomb. However, in a shotgun, the energy of combustion initially is transferred to a single entity that then dissipates into the individual pellets only after leaving the barrel.

3. ANFO is a powerful explosive mixture containing ammonium nitrate and fuel oil. It was used in the 1995 bombing of the Federal Building in Oklahoma City. Optimal power, related to Q, is obtained with a mixture of ~94% NH$_4$NO$_3$ and 6% fuel oil. What is the approximate oxygen balance of fuel oil?

Optimum power is reached when the combined oxygen balance is 0. This quantity for NH$_4$NO$_3$ can be calculated based on the balanced equation of combustion, here assuming simple gaseous products:

$$NH_4NO_3 \rightarrow N_2 + 2H_2O + 1/2O_2$$

To calculate the oxygen balance, which is positive, use equation 9.12:

$$\text{Oxygen balance} = \frac{\frac{1}{2}\text{mole} * 16\frac{g}{\text{mole}}}{1\,\text{mole} * 80\frac{g}{\text{mole}}} * 100 = 10\%$$

This is a fairly low positive oxygen balance, so it is not surprising that there is a large amount of this solid needed to make up for the expected large negative oxygen balance of fuel oil, which consists principally of hydrocarbons. The calculation is completed by substitution similar to that shown in Figure 9.12:

$$0.94(10) + 0.06x = 0$$
$$9.4 + 0.06x = 0$$
$$x = -9.4/0.06 = -157$$
$$\text{Check by } 9.4 + 0.06\,(-157) = 0$$

This result presents a bit of a quandary, since the definition of oxygen balance is based on a percentage and would be expected to fall between 1 and 100. Recall however, that this type of calculation is an estimate and what it tells us is in line with what we expected; mixtures of hydrocarbons such as fuel oil will have very little oxygen to contribute to any explosion. Also, recall that some oxygen will be available from the atmosphere.

4. Determine if reactions 9-14 through 9-18 are exothermic or endothermic under standard conditions. For each predict how the system will respond to:

This problem is no longer valid

5.

a) Methane explosions can destroy homes. Assume that a natural gas furnace is located in an enclosed basement room with dimensions of 8' x 6' x 8'. A leak begins and methane is introduced into the room at a rate of 100 grams per hour. The flammability limits of methane are approximately 0.5 to 1.6. If the pressure in the room is one atmosphere and the temperature is 18°C, how long before the methane concentration reaches a flammable stage?

There are two ways to approach this problem. One is iteratively and graphically; the other is by calculation. Assumptions are that the room is closed and leak tight and that a homogeneous mixture is achieved. As such, the time is a best case estimate and the longest a leak would have to continue. Since methane will rise, there will be a region in which a combustible mixture forms sooner than in the case of the assumed homogeneous mixture.

Start by putting all units in proper format for the ideal gas law; volume of the room = 384 ft³ or 10,874 L and 70°F = 294K. The flammability limits are Φ = 0.5 to 1.6 and we'll use 29 g mol⁻¹ as the weighted average mass of air. Although there are several ways to approach this problem, a reasonable and relatively easy way is to use a spreadsheet and the equations and relationships presented in Example Problem 9.4. As seen in the following table, a "what if" scenario works well to answer this question as well as part b below:

moles of methane	$P_{methane}$	P_{total}	$X_{methane}$	X_{air}	Ratio	Hours
50.0	0.111	1.000	0.111	0.889	14.5	8.0
100.0	0.222	1.000	0.222	0.778	6.4	16.0
150.0	0.333	1.000	0.333	0.667	3.6	24.0
200.0	0.444	1.000	0.444	0.556	2.3	32.0
225.0	0.499	1.000	0.499	0.501	1.8	36.0
235.0	0.522	1.000	0.522	0.478	1.7	37.6
240.0	**0.533**	**1.000**	**0.533**	**0.467**	**1.6**	**38.4**
250.0	0.555	1.000	0.555	0.445	1.5	40.0
300.0	0.666	1.000	0.666	0.334	0.9	48.0
350.0	**0.777**	**1.000**	**0.777**	**0.223**	**0.5**	**56.0**
400.0	0.888	1.000	0.888	0.112	0.2	64.0
450.0	0.999	1.000	0.999	0.001	0.0	72.0
Part b:						
50.0	0.111	0.890	0.125	0.875	12.7	8.0
100.0	0.222	0.890	0.249	0.751	5.5	16.0
150.0	0.333	0.890	0.374	0.626	3.0	24.0
200.0	0.444	0.890	0.499	0.501	1.8	32.0
213.0	**0.473**	**0.890**	**0.531**	**0.469**	**1.6**	**34.1**
225.0	0.499	0.890	0.561	0.439	1.4	36.0
250.0	0.555	0.890	0.624	0.376	1.1	40.0
300.0	0.666	0.890	0.748	0.252	0.6	48.0
310.0	**0.688**	**0.890**	**0.773**	**0.227**	**0.5**	**49.6**
325.0	0.721	0.890	0.811	0.189	0.4	52.0
350.0	0.777	0.890	0.873	0.127	0.3	56.0
400.0	0.888	0.890	0.998	0.002	0.0	64.0

Note that by bracketing the desired values and adding lines, it is possible to zero in on when the flammability range is reached, here between ~38 and 56 hours. The first four quantities are calculated as in the example problem; the hours needed are calculated by first converting the moles of methane to grams and dividing by the rate of 100 grams hour^{-1}, leaving a result in hours.

b) The same scenario occurs in a home located in the mountains of New Mexico, where the atmospheric pressure is approximately 0.89 atmospheres. How does this change the scenario? Justify and explain.

Using the spreadsheet approach as shown above, flammability is reached faster. This makes sense since at a lower total atmospheric pressure, the relative concentration of propane is higher. The same concept applies to any solution; if you add a set amount of solute to a larger total volume, the concentration of that solute is lower than if a smaller total volume is used.

c) Based on material shown in Figure 9.24, how would this change your interpretation of the data?

(Note the error in Figure number) Methane is lighter than air, with a formula weight of 16 compared with the weighted average of 29 g mol^{-1}. As a result, in a sealed room, methane will collect toward the ceiling and will reach a combustible stage faster at higher elevations in the room. Thus, location of the ignition source would have to be taken into consideration; if high in the room, combustibility is reached sooner than if the ignition source is lower in the room.

6. Two common solvents used in clandestine drug labs are diethyl ether and acetone. Being less than vigilant in lab and safety practices, clandestine chemists often work with leaky equipment. If a person was brought to the emergency room under suspicious circumstances, where would you predict the burn patterns on their body to be most pronounced if they were injured by a fire/explosion at a clandestine laboratory?

The damage would likely be on the lower extremities since both solvents are denser than air. The formula weight of diethyl ether is 64 g/mole and the weight of acetone is 58 g/mole, compared with 29 for air.

7. A temperature above the flashpoint of a fuel is a necessary condition for combustion, but is it a sufficient one?

No, the mixture must still be in the flammable range and have the proper F/A ratio to support combustion.

8. Based on the results of part a, Example Problem 9.6, comment on the oxygen balance of nitroglycerin.

Error in this numbering, refer instead to Problem 9.5. Recall that we already calculated the oxygen balance for this molecule in Example Problem 9.3. Note how Problem 9.5 shows how the excess oxygen is used and why it is important in dictating the final mixture of products.

9.

    a) Use the Springall Roberts rules (Table 9.5) to predict the products of the explosion of TNT.

This problem can be approached using fractions, but to simplify, note that fractions of 1/3 and 1/6 are used in this rule set. Thus, to lessen the use of fractions and the accompanying risk of error, start with six molecules of TNT and proceed as shown in the figures

TNT = $6C_7H_5N_3O_6$ = 42C, 30H, 18N, 36O

Rule ①

42CO
Requires 42O
so none is left
of the original 36

Rules ② and ③ don't apply

④

9N$_2$

⑤

1/3 of 42 = 14CO$_2$
leaves 28CO

⑥

28CO − 7CO = 21CO left

1/6 of 42 = 7CO

7C   7H$_2$O
          Which requires 14H
          30H (original) − 14 = 16H = 8H$_2$

Collect terms
$$6C_7H_5N_3O_6 \longrightarrow 21CO + 14CO_2 + 7C + 7H_2O + 8H_2 + 9N_2$$
Double check, omitting oxygen

Since we know there is a deficit:
$$42C \longrightarrow 21 + 14 + 7 = 42C$$
$$30H \longrightarrow 14H + 16H = 30H$$
$$18N \longrightarrow 18N$$
Note how avoiding the fractions made this easier.

b) If 1.00 gram of TNT is detonated, what is the total volume of gas is produced?

Use the results from part a above and note that the detonation of 6 moles of TNT produces all gaseous products except for the solid carbon; the total number of moles of gas is 21 + 14 + 7 + 8 + 9 = 59 per 6 moles of TNT or 9.8 moles gas per mole TNT. The formula weight of TNT is 227 g mol^{-1} so 1 gram of TNT is equivalent to 0.004 moles:

0.004 moles TNT * 9.8 moles gas (mol TNT^{-1}) = 0.043 moles gas * 22.4 L mol^{1} at STP = 0.97 L

c) How much heat is produced?

Lots, calculate using $\Delta H°_{rxn} = \Sigma[\Delta H°]_{products} - \Sigma[\Delta H°]_{reactants}$ as we have done many times before. The contribution of elemental products C, H_2, and N_2 can be ignored since their values are 0. This leaves:

$\Delta H°_{rxn} = [21*\Delta H°CO + 14\Delta H°CO_2 + 7\Delta H°H_2O] - 6[\Delta H°TNT]$ all units in kJ mol and assuming all products are in the gaseous phase. The heat of formation of TNT is available in the CRC Handbook and leads to:

$\Delta H°_{rxn} = [21(-110.5) + 14(-393.5) + 7(-241.82)] - 6[-63.2] = [-9522.2] + 379.2 = -9143$ kJ

This is for 6 moles of TNT, so per mole, ~1524 kJ are released or per gram, ~6.7 kJ.

10. Crude bombs can be made from dry ice. How do they work and what type of chemical evidence would be left behind if one were used?

The pressure wave is a result of the rapid vaporization and expansion of solid CO_2 to the gaseous product, which is a physical change (phase change) as opposed to a chemical change such as a detonation. There would be no chemical residual left behind, a fact that would be critical by itself. There would also have to be some device or mechanism to transport the dry ice and keep it cold until ready to detonate; a heat source would also be expected to make certain that the volatization was rapid enough to breech whatever container the dry ice was placed in.

Integrative

1. TATP (triacetone triperixoide, $C_9H_{18}O_6$), is an extremely powerful and sensitive explosive first made in the late 1800s.

    a) Find the structure of this material.

    See at right.

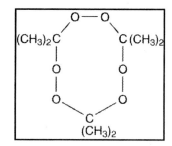

    b) Calculate the value of $\Delta H°$ for the complete combustion of TATP at stoichiometric equivalence.

First balance the combustion equation, here assuming the products are CO_2 and H_2O:

$$2C_9H_{18}O_6 + 21O_2 \rightarrow 18CO_2 + 18H_2O$$

The CRC Handbook does not list the $\Delta H°$ for the formation of TATP, so the bond-breaking and formation method will be used here. In table form and using the balanced equation:

Broken	Number	kJ each	Total	Formed	Number	kJ each	Total
C-H	36	413	14686	C=O	36	799	28764
C-C	12	348	4176	H-O	36	463	16668
C-O	12	358	4296			Total:	45432
O-O	6	146	876				
O=O	21	495	10395				
		Total:	36411			Net Q:	10821

The approximate $\Delta H°_{rxn}$ = -10821 kJ as written above or 5411kJ per mole of TATP detonated.

    c) How many moles of gaseous products would be produced by the explosion of 10.0 g of TATP?

FW TATP = 222 g mol^{-1} so 10.0 grams = 0.045 moles of TATP. Using mole ratios and the balanced equation, this would produce:

$$\boxed{\text{Moles CO}_2 = 0.45 \text{ moles TATP} * \frac{18 \text{ moles CO}_2}{2 \text{ moles TATP}} = 4.05 \text{ moles CO}_2}$$

Moles of gaseous water are the same so the total moles of gas produced by the detonation of 10.0 g of TATP would be 8.10 = 8.1 moles or ~181 liters at STP.

d) What would the IR of this material look like (roughly)? Assign bands and intensities. What features common to other explosives are noticeably absent?

One of the interesting things about the peroxide explosives is the relative lack of spectral detail and features. The O-O absorbance is relatively weak and no carbonyl absorbance band is present. The only features of interest above the fingerprint region would be weak bands associated with the methyl groups in the 3000 cm^{-1} region.

2. How do silencers work? Would the use of a silencer impart changes in the physical evidence left by firing it compared with a non-silenced weapon?

The role of a silencer is to reduce sound that is created by the pressure waves generated by the burning of the propellant. To achieve this, silencers are devices that attach to the barrel of a weapon and that may extend back over it some distance. Gases are directed into the device, which usually consists of some type of baffling system that serves to disrupt and slow the gases before they exit the weapon. Since a silencer is attached to the barrel, it will inevitably capture some of the GSR. Additionally, if the bullet passes through a tube that is part of the silencer, toolmarks can be left on the bullet that are not attributable to the barrel alone.

Food for thought

1. Hydrogen is billed as "the fuel of the future" for automobiles. A popular misconception, mostly due to films of the *Hindenburg* disaster, is that cars that store hydrogen as fuel will be more likely to explode in an accident than current cars using gasoline. Why is this a misconception?

Hydrogen is far less dense than air and if spilled or otherwise spilled from a breached container, it would rapidly dissipate, moving up and away from the source of the leak. The timeframe and location in which a combustible mixture would exist would be limited compared with a gasoline leak.

Combustion II: Forensic Analysis of Physical Evidence Associated With Combustion	CHAPTER 10

From the chapter

1. Is SPME destructive or nondestructive? Justify.

It is somewhere between depending on how it is used. A SPME will remove target analytes, here hydrocarbons and accelerants from the matrix and destroy them. However, since the technique requires much less sample than a comparable technique such as solvent extraction, it is unlikely that any one extraction will remove all of the volatiles of interest. Ideally, only a representative subset will be removed.

2. Is the environment experienced by brake linings similar to that which produces GSR? Why or why not? How would you respond on the stand to a challenge to GSR identification based on the possibility of such a false positive?

Like the interior of a weapon during the firing event, brake linings can become very hot when brakes are applied. However, the heat is the result of friction and not combustion, an important difference. As was discussed in Exhibit B, the morphology of GSR particulates is different than that of particulates formed in brake linings which would be expected based on the different ways in which they form. Also, brake linings have many other ingredients, while the Ba-Sb-Pb and associated combinations to date are generally considered unique to GSR.

Integrative

1. Comment on the similarities between the presumptive tests for GSR shown in Figures 10.10–12 and those described for drugs in Chapter 7. What are the common threads?

The common themes are formations of azo dye compounds, coupling reactions, and exploitation of transition metal complexes as part of the tests for lead and barium. The colored products are all highly conjugated systems.

Food for thought

1. Can you make a bomb using only dry ice? How?

Yes, simply place a large amount of dry ice in a relatively thick container and heat it rapidly. There is no explosion, but there is a rapid expansion of hot gas produced from the solid that can rupture a container, creating a bomb.

Dyes and Pigments, Inks and Paints: Analytical Chemistry and Colorants

From the chapter

1. Methyl orange is a dye and acid/base indicator. Locate the structure and classify this dye based on the systems presented in this chapter.

Methyl orange is an azo dye and also an anionic dye.

2. Examine Table 11.2 and rationalize the values in light of their definitions.

In this case, the XYZ values represent the contributions of blue, green, and red, respectively, to a spectrum of a light source. Both of these sources are meant to mimic natural light with D50 representing indoor lighting and D65 representing outdoor daylight. Both are dominated by green light, but the relative contribution of red is higher for indoor lighting compared with typical outdoor lighting.

3. What is the difference between solvent evaporation, curing, and drying?

Evaporation is strictly a physical phase change in which the solvent evaporates from the liquid to the gaseous state.

4. What is the core structure of a Rhodamine colorant?

Actually there are several features of interest, but the core is a series of rings, two aromatics joined by an oxygenated ring. There are also two amino groups.

5. Given the following data for a visible spectrum of an ink, derive the tristimulus values. What color is the ink? What dyes or pigments shown in the tables in this chapter might be responsible assuming that a single colorant is used?

λ	R (%)
400	10.0
420	12.0
440	8.0
460	12.0
480	19.0
500	65.0
520	75.0
540	65.0
560	65.0
580	22.0
600	12.0
620	10.0
640	5.0
660	4.0
680	6.0
700	2.0

Plotting the spectrum is an easy way to predict color. As seen at the right, reflectance in the green range is strong and so this ink will appear to be some shade of green.

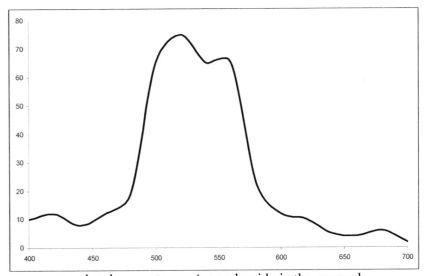

Deriving the tristimulus values is best accomplished using a spreadsheet, the same one use to plot the spectrum. A good guide is the example calculation in the text and in the Appendix. Using that algorithm and those values for observer curves and illuminants, the following spreadsheet is derived:

λ	R	x	y	z	C	C*y	X	Y	Z
380	0.10	0.001	0.000	0.007	26.59	0.00	0.00	0.00	0.02
390	0.10	0.004	0.000	0.020	38.20	0.00	0.02	0.00	0.08
400	0.10	0.014	0.000	0.068	51.01	0.02	0.07	0.00	0.35
410	0.11	0.044	0.001	0.207	64.95	0.08	0.31	0.01	1.48
420	0.12	0.134	0.004	0.646	79.06	0.32	1.28	0.04	6.12
430	0.10	0.284	0.012	1.386	90.58	1.05	2.57	0.11	12.55
440	0.08	0.348	0.023	1.747	97.91	2.25	2.73	0.18	13.69
450	0.10	0.336	0.038	1.772	99.93	3.80	3.36	0.38	17.71
460	0.12	0.291	0.060	1.669	99.20	5.95	3.46	0.71	19.87
470	0.16	0.195	0.091	1.288	99.77	9.08	3.02	1.41	19.91
480	0.19	0.096	0.139	0.813	99.85	13.88	1.81	2.64	15.42
490	0.42	0.032	0.208	0.465	97.27	20.23	1.31	8.50	19.00
500	0.65	0.005	0.323	0.272	90.34	29.18	0.29	18.97	15.97
510	0.70	0.009	0.503	0.158	82.44	41.47	0.54	29.03	9.13
520	0.75	0.063	0.710	0.078	78.09	55.44	3.71	41.58	4.58
530	0.70	0.166	0.862	0.042	78.97	68.08	9.15	47.65	2.33
540	0.65	0.290	0.954	0.020	82.28	78.49	15.53	51.02	1.09
550	0.65	0.433	0.995	0.009	84.78	84.35	23.88	54.83	0.48
560	0.65	0.595	0.995	0.004	84.86	84.43	32.79	54.88	0.22
570	0.44	0.762	0.952	0.002	82.44	78.48	27.33	34.14	0.08
580	0.22	0.916	0.870	0.002	78.81	68.57	15.89	15.08	0.03
590	0.17	1.026	0.757	0.001	75.11	56.86	13.10	9.67	0.01
600	0.12	0.180	0.631	0.001	72.29	45.61	1.56	5.47	0.01
610	0.11	0.190	0.503	0.000	71.24	35.83	1.49	3.94	0.00
620	0.10	0.200	0.381	0.000	71.00	27.05	1.42	2.70	0.00
630	0.08	0.220	0.265	0.000	70.92	18.79	1.17	1.41	0.00
640	0.05	0.230	0.175		70.76	12.38	0.81	0.62	0.00
650	0.05	0.284	0.107		71.08	7.61	0.91	0.34	0.00
660	0.04	0.165	0.061		70.84	4.32	0.47	0.17	0.00
670	0.05	0.087	0.032		69.55	2.23	0.30	0.11	0.00
680	0.06	0.047	0.017		67.69	1.15	0.19	0.07	0.00
690	0.04	0.023	0.008		64.63	0.53	0.06	0.02	0.00
700	0.02	0.011	0.004		61.49	0.25	0.01	0.01	0.00
710	0.02	0.006	0.002		58.34	0.12	0.01	0.00	0.00
720	0.02	0.003	0.001		55.04	0.06	0.00	0.00	0.00
730	0.02	0.001	0.001		51.90	0.03	0.00	0.00	0.00
740	0.02	0.001	0.000			0	0	0	0
750	0.02	0.000	0.000			0	0	0	0
760	0.02	0.000	0.000			0	0	0	0
770	0.00	0.000	0.000			0	0	0	0

Points to note: First, where no data was provided for reflectance (here as a fraction of 1.00), linear extrapolation was used except on the ends, where same values were substituted. The 1931

CIE values were used and using the procedures outlined in the text (equations 11.4–11.9), the following tristimulus values and chromaticity coordinates were obtained:

X	Y	Z
170.6	385.7	160.1
19.9	45.0	18.7

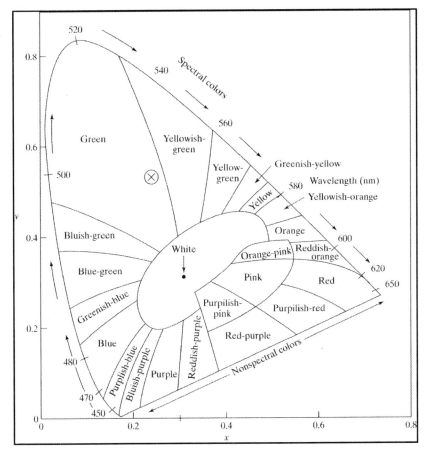

The chromaticity coordinates are x = 0.24 and y = 0.54.

The coordinates fall within the green range as expected.

6. Review the structures of some of the dyes and pigments presented in this chapter. Are there any that would *not* show some absorbance in the IR range?

No, all would be active and have a spectrum.

7. Melamine polymers are becoming more common in paints and inks. What are they and how do they form a protective film? What else are these polymeric materials used for?

Melamines are a subgroup of polymers formed by the reaction of formaldehyde and melamine. This type of polymer is called a condensation polymer, a topic discussed in detail in Chapter 13. Figure 13.33 shows the formation of a melamine polymer. These materials are used as coatings for cars, among other applications.

8. Applying the Science 11.1 discusses the polymerization of pigments in wine.

a) How do the structures shown in the sidebar compare with those given in Tables 11.3 and 11.4?

Note the correction of table reference. The key features of dyes/pigments are linked conjugated systems, which are also the heart of the wine colorants shown in this sidebar.

b) Refer back to the Marquis test discussed in Chapter 7 and comment on the similarities.

Figures 7.13–7.15 illustrate formation of colored materials upon reaction with the Marquis reagent (sulfuric acid and formaldehyde). A striking similarity is the polymerization step that generates a larger conjugated system, a key step in creating color.

Integrative

1. Why are the orange and red dyes typically smaller molecules than the blue dyes? Relate to the fundamental principles of color.

It is because they absorb in the blue range, which reflects higher energies of transition relative to compounds that absorb in the red and orange range (appearing blue). The more highly conjugated and generally (but not always) larger the molecule, the lower the energy required to effect the electronic transition.

2. Based on the discussion in Chapter 7 and the material in the Appendix, predict λ_{max} and the color of the dyes Sudan III, Tartrazine, and Fat Brown.

Note the correction to wording; structures are found in an Appendix. All three contain extended conjugated systems that defy simple applications of the Woodward-Fieser rules. Sudan II has the longest conjugated system. Tartrazine (CI Food Yellow 13) is yellow; Sudan III is CI Solvent Red 23, and Fat Brown is actually a family of dyes, mostly red in color. To explain these colors, consideration of donor and acceptor groups is useful. Groups such as –OH, amines, and acetates donate electrons to the conjugated systems, resulting in energy levels that are on average closer together. Receptor groups include sulfites as seen in the tartrazine system. When both donors and acceptors are present, more resonance structures exist, reducing the size of the energy gaps.

Source: Nassau, K.. *The Physics and Chemistry of Color* 2nd Edition. New York: John Wiley and Sons; 2001. Ch. 6: Color in Organic Molecules; p. 113–142.

3. Drugs and dyes share at least two general similarities as a group of compounds. Discuss.

Both classes of compounds include acids, bases, and neutrals and the basic compounds are nitrogenous bases.

4. Locate the structure of chlorophyll and categorize it. Might this substance be found in items of physical evidence? Suggest an analytical scheme to identify it.

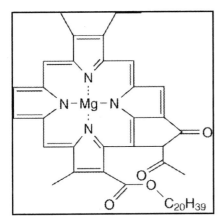

This pigment is similar to the copper-based phthalocyanine structures with magnesium as the complexing metal rather than copper. There are actually several chlorophylls and what is shown is chlorophyll a. The hydrocarbon attachment ($C_{20}H_{39}$) consists of an extensive conjugated system. Since chlorophylls are in plant matter, their presence in many kinds of physical evidence is expected. What differentiates chlorophyll from other green colorants is the presence of the magnesium; this would be a logical target for analysis. Elemental techniques would be of use here, but also the traditional spectroscopic techniques, particularly vibrational (IR and Raman),

5. An older resin system used in automotive paints exploited cellulosic-based resins such as nitrocellulose. What are the components of this resin system? How does the film form?

We saw this material previously in Chapter 9 in the context of propellants. Nitrocellulose resins are made by treating cellulose (cotton or wood pulp) with concentrated HNO_3 and H_2SO_4. The acids drive esterification (polymerization) and nitration of some of the –OH groups. Guncotton has the highest percentage of nitrogen by weight, ~12–14%, whereas the materials used as lacquers and coatings have lower nitrogen content, in the range of 11–12%.

Source: Allcock, H. R., et al. *Contemporary Polymer Chemistry* 3rd Edition. Upper Saddle River, NJ: Pearson/Prentice Hall; 2003. Ch. 13: Biopolymers; p. 191–228.

Food for thought

1. Why are white boards (Dry-Erase boards) nonporous? For writing on such boards, what type of dyes/pigments and solvents would be best? Would special additives be needed? For what purpose? Justify your answer.

It is to avoid having the ink soak into them. If the inks penetrate the surface, they cannot be wiped away. The best solvents are those that evaporate very slowly and that do not have any film-forming capability (i.e., those that do not polymerize). The types of additives expected would be those that prevent any type of penetration and that hinder drying.

2. What do tristimulus values and principle component analysis (Chapter 3) have in common?

Principal components are used to generate linear combinations of variables that can capture the most variance in a data set and that can be used to reduce the dimensionality of a data set. Tristimulus values are similar in that they use weighting factors (analogous to factor weights) to reduce the dimensionality of a spectrum from 300 data points to 2 in the form of chromaticity coordinates.

<table>
<tr><td>

Forensic Analysis of Inks and Paints

</td><td>

CHAPTER
12

</td></tr>
</table>

From the chapter

1. Why are pigments typically more difficult to analyze using chromatographic techniques such as TLC than dyes?

This is because of solubility. By definition, a pigment is not soluble in the solvent used to deliver it; most of these solvents are the same ones used in TLC and HPLC as well as in sample preparation for GC.

2. How does the complimentary relationship of FTIR and Raman spectroscopy enhance the analysis of inks and paints?

Although both IR and Raman probe vibrational modes, the interactions arise in fundamentally different ways and can thus provide different types of information. Bonds that are not amenable to IR interaction are usually Raman active and vice versa, providing a more complete understanding of the vibrational interactions found in the sampled area. In addition, Raman is typically a surface analysis, while IR can be a surface or a transmission analysis. This is useful in cases such as fibers or inks on a substrate in which information about both is desired. The drawback to this approach is the limited sensitivity of Raman relative to IR.

3. List and discuss some of the caveats and limitations of artificial aging studies such as those discussed and shown in Figure 12.11.

The key limitation is summed up in the name *artificial*. The environment that an exhibit of evidence has experienced over its lifetime can never be accurately reproduced and the number of variables is considerable. These include lighting, temperature, and atmospheric conditions to name just a few. Another consideration is the interaction between the ink and the substrate, also something that cannot be exactly reproduced.

Integrative

1. Which dye molecules would be amenable to typical GCMS methods and which would not? Why?

To be amenable to GCMS methods, a compound must be volatile at ~300°C, must be soluble in a solvent that can be used in GCMS, and must have a molecular weight range that the mass spectrometer is capable of scanning, typically 500 amu or less. Finally, the molecule must not be sensitive to thermal degradation. The last consideration is the least important relative to GCMS analysis of dyes.

Examination of the representative structures in Tables 11.4 and 11.5 illustrates how these criteria can be applied. Benzidine yellow has a molecular weight of 629.5 amu and has a melting point of ~320°C and thus would not be amenable to GCMS. Indanthren blue is smaller at ~442 amu, but is practically insoluble in all organic solvents. The quinacridones have similar solubility limitations. Of all the examples provided in Table 11.4, solvent red 1 is the only one that might be amenable to GCMS based on formula weight and solubility; indigo (Table 11.5) also falls into this category.

A good source of information for this type of question is the Hazardous Substances Database available online through the National Library of Medicine gateway, currently (mid-2005) found at http://chem2.sis.nlm.nih.gov/chemidplus/chemidlite.jsp. Enter the compound name and the search results will include a link to the HSDB. In that database, there is a summary of chemical and physical properties that includes formula weight and some solubility data.

2. In fire debris analysis, weathering is manifest by an increase in chromatographic peaks with relatively higher molecular weights, whereas in ink evidence, weathering is manifest by a shift to lower molecular weights. Why?

In fire debris, the trend is created by weathering and evaporation, processes that favor the lighter materials over the heavier. As weathering progresses, losses progress from the lighter to the heavier, which is reflected chromatographically by a shift to patterns of higher molecular weight composition. In contrast, the weathering or aging process (except very early on; see question 1 in

Food for thought below) is a process of degradation driven principally by exposure to UV radiation. The larger molecules that make up the binders, polymerized agents, and so on break down to smaller molecules. Thus, it is the specific mechanism of the weathering and the timeframe over which it occurs that dictates the resulting chromatographic patterns.

Food for thought

1. Why are solvents used in inks and paints usually of less forensic interest than the binders and colorants?

They are of less interest because they are the first components to be lost as a result of wear and weathering. Unlike fire debris evidence, ink and paint evidence is rarely fresh and even if it is, solvent formulations are typically not as useful as colorants and binder composition for which there are databases of information available.

The Chemistry of Polymers

From the chapter

1. Why is the term *anhydroglucose* used to describe glucose polymers? What classification of polymer does this place cellulose in?

This is because their formation involves the loss of water; this would place them in the category of condensation polymer.

2. Provide the chemical explanation for why lignin would be expected to contribute to the acidity of paper. What other groups are involved and how does the bound water in paper (Figure 13.17) contribute?

Note the correction of figure number. There is an –OH group in the chain between the two benzene rings that could be acidic. The water could contribute H+ and could stabilize the protonation.

3. Most papers lose their strength when wet. What is the chemical explanation for this?

An excess of water will weaken the hydrogen bonds between the fibers as they hydrogen bond with the water instead.

4. Based on the characteristics of cellulose, what group(s) of dyes would be appropriate for dying cotton and paper aside from those already discussed? Explain based on intermolecular forces such as ion-ion, ion-dipole, etc.

The available functionality are the exposed –OH groups, which could participate in covalent bonding and in electrostatic bonding if protonated. Dyes that associate via hydrogen bonding would also be appropriate.

5. In 2002, Cargill Dow introduced a new synthetic fiber labeled PLA and made from lactic acid monomers. What are the characteristics of this fiber? How is it made? How is it similar to cellulose?

PLA stands for polylactic acid and it is made as the name implies. The structure of this polymer includes exposed end groups –OH and repeating units that include an –O– bond. This facilitates hydrogen bonding as in cellulose.

6. Kevlar is relatively easy to identify. Why?

The cross-linking makes for a strong fiber in contrast with other nylons; it has a highly ordered structure and many functional groups that are IR active.

7. *This problem is no longer valid*

Integrative

1. An older color-based presumptive test for saliva is based on the presence of the enzyme amylase. It employs starch gel and iodine in an interesting way. Explain how this test is performed, its chemical basis, and its limitations. How is this test related to material presented in this chapter?

This test was performed by making a starch gel and pouring it into a Petri dish to set up. Holes were then punched in the gel and suspected saliva sample extracts placed in the wells. Overnight, the samples diffused radially outward from the well. The next day, the gel was immersed in an iodine solution. If the sample well contained saliva and thus amylase, the enzyme would have broken down the starch in the gel, preventing it from reacting with the iodine to form the characteristic deep blue start-iodine (I_3^-) complex. The larger the clear zone around a well, the more amylase was present.

2. Describe and discuss similarities and differences between the helical conformation of amylose and the helical structure of DNA. What fundamental chemical principals and intermolecular forces lead to these conformations?

Hydrogen bonding is the common thread that facilitates helical structures. In amylose, the structure forms helices in water and all of the subunits are the same. DNA contains different units and two strands rather than one.

3. Locate a reference that describes sample preparation in entomotoxicology. What approach is used to breakdown chitin?

Chitin is typically broken down by an enzymatic degradation.

4. From your knowledge of the structure of glucose and cellulose, identify which groups are infrared absorbers. Where in the spectrum would most IR spectral features be expected to appear? Locate or obtain an IR spectrum of cellulose and correlate absorbances to chemical functionality.

Actually, not many groups are infrared absorbers. The –OH absorbance will be strong along with C-H activity and C-O bands. Depending on the conditions and source, these bands will be easily identified using the information in Appendix 4.

5. A question from the previous chapter dealt with the indicator phenolphthalein that is also used in a common presumptive test for blood. If a typical sheet of office paper is slightly wetted, what color would phenolphthalein likely appear? From the perspective of using it for a presumptive test for blood, is there a possibility for interference?

Modern office paper is acid free or at least treated with buffers, so it will probably not change color and would remain colorless.

6. Could the cation exchange capacity of paper be used to characterize it? Why or why not? What variables would have to be controlled?

Perhaps, but moisture content would have to be tightly controlled since this is critical in determining access to active sites

7. A simple TLC experiment can be performed in which water soluble inks are applied to filter paper and the chromatogram developed using water as the solvent. Explain what interactions in the paper allow for separation to occur. Examine the various dye classes and predict how each as a class would be expected to behave under these chromatographic conditions.

Paper has polar functionality in the –OH groups that will interact with polar dyes. The only dyes that would not interact would be those that are nonpolar or nearly so. Examples would include some of the anthraquinones.

8. How is the process of dyeing a fiber similar to the processes that occur in chromatography? How is it similar to movement of ions in solution to an electrode surface?

Both processes involve partitioning between two phases, the solvent "mobile" phase and the fiber. If the dye is charged (cation/anion) and a bond forms at the surface, this is quite similar to species moving toward an electrode; similar double layers would be expected to form.

Food for thought

1. Why are white boards (Dry-Erase boards) nonporous? For writing on such boards, what type of dyes/pigments and solvents would be best? Justify.

They are nonporous so the colorant will not seep into the board, making it difficult to wipe away. Pigments would be ideal since they remain on the surface.

2. Why would a bicomponent fiber be considered to have strong evidentiary value?

because they are still somewhat unusual

<table>
<tr><td>

The Forensic Analysis of Paper, Fibers, and Polymers

</td><td>

CHAPTER

14

</td></tr>
</table>

From the chapter

1. Based on the element list presented for the ICP-MS discrimination of papers approach, what would some of the practical problems be related to sample preparation? In other words, how would the analyst be confident that the element concentrations measured were attributed to the paper matrix and not incidental or contaminants?

The first step would be to assure that the elements detected originate from within the paper matrix itself and not from contaminants on the surface. Elements such as sodium and magnesium are common and are easily transferred from skin to paper. Handling with gloves would be the first step, followed by a surface cleaning that is sufficiently aggressive to remove contaminants from the surface without stripping elemental constituents from the internal matrix. If such a protocol is too involved or complex, the more common elements might be best eliminated from the study.

By focusing on the trace elements such as Sr, Y, Ba, La, and Ce, issues of contamination and carryover could be reduced, but the cost paid will be in uncertainty and precision. At these much lower detection limits (Figure 14.1), the %RSD of the results will be expected to be much larger, necessitating a comprehensive sampling plan that includes replicates.

2. How do delustering treatments such as placing particulates of TiO_2 on a fiber surface decrease shine?

We perceive shine when light is reflected directly back as in specular reflection. Adding particulates such as TiO_2 cause scattering and diffuse reflection, while decreasing specular reflection and shiny appearance.

3. A case examination reveals the following fibers on a piece of evidence. Rank them in order of likely relative evidentiary importance and justify.

Number	Type	Color	Length
1	Viscose rayon	Black	3.1 mm
2	Cotton	White	7.2 mm
3	Cotton	Orange	0.2mm
4	Dacron	Green	5.1 mm
5	Wool	White	<0.2 mm
6	Triacetate	Orange	4.2 mm
7	Polyamide	Red	2 mm

The factors of interest here are fiber length and color. Longer fibers are more likely the result of a recent transfer relative to shorter fibers since such large fibers will be easier to dislodge relative to shorter fibers. The more unusual the color, the less likely the fiber is to be found in the normal "background" of fibers. Accordingly, the orange fibers are more likely to allow for discrimination than white fibers. Finally, fiber type must be considered. Cotton is a common fiber type and would typically carry less evidentiary weight, all else being equal.

This problem presents a purposeful challenge by mixing these criteria and as such it is more appropriate to group fibers by likely importance rather than set out a single ordered list. The green Dacron, white cotton, and black rayon, because of length and color, would warrant careful evaluation., as would the orange triacetate fiber. The orange cotton would merit attention because of the unusual color. At the lower end of the importance scale would be the red nylon and white wool. Keep in mind that as a hypothetical case, many factors cannot be included in the discussion.

4. A PBT polyester fiber has a symmetrical dumbbell cross-section with a maximum thickness of 80μm and a minimum of 40μm. Describe how this fiber would appear under crossed polars (maximum interference colors).

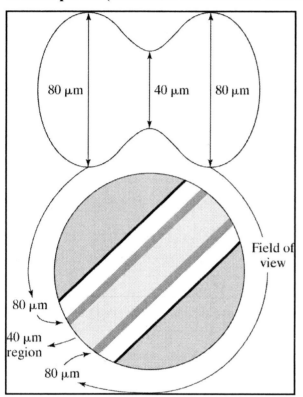

First, as per Table 14.4, note that PBT polyester is strongly birefringent and will exhibit bright colors at 45°. As shown in the figure to the left, the fiber would appear to have a bright band down the middle corresponding to the thin middle section and then two dark bands symmetrically placed on either side of the light band. Each of these side areas would have the same banding pattern as a cylindrical fiber.

5. Suppose you were to observe a nylon fiber under cross polars while the fiber was gradually heated to its melting point. Describe what you would see.

Nylon is pseudocrystalline and would be predicted to roughly follow the behavior illustrated in Figure 13.5. PLM, in effect, monitors the degree of crystallinity of the fiber and the degree of difference between the refractive index in the parallel and perpendicular directions. As the heat is increased, the crystalline structure begins to degrade. As such, the birefringence will decrease and the interference colors will slowly fade back toward the grays and blacks. Eventually, when the fiber approaches the liquid state, there will be no organized structure and the fiber will no longer be visible under crossed polars.

6. If a case involved a single nylon fiber as crucial evidence, what tests would you select for the analysis and why? How would this change if you had 20 fibers (all similar)?

When sample is limited, the only options are nondestructive tests such as polarizing light microscopy and microspectrophotometry such as ATR or other type of IR, UV/VIS, and Raman. Interestingly, having 20+ fibers would likely not change the analytical approach significantly. It would allow for dye analysis using chromatographic techniques such as TLC and GCMS, but such techniques would not necessarily add significantly to the amount of information produced.

Integrative

1. Research how paper is recycled and comment on how the process(es) will impact the chemical characterization of paper. Should there be ways to distinguish recycled paper from nonrecycled? Among recycled batches? Present answers in three analytical areas: microscopic/visual analysis, organic, and inorganic.

In general, the process for making paper from old paper is similar to that used to make paper from wood chips as starting material. The added steps involve sorting the starting materials, isolation of useable fibers, contaminant removal, de-inking by solvent treatments, and bleaching. De-inking is a complex process given the variety of ways in which ink can be applied to paper. Ink is much like paint and can contain dyes, pigments, and film forming agents. Colorants applied via a thermal setting as in laser printing and copying contain waxes and adhesives that must also be removed from the recycled materials.

Recycled paper would be expected to contain, on average, shorter fibers than nonrecycled paper because of the added mechanical steps. Residuals of inks may remain and unbleached recycled paper has an off-white color. Recycled paper may not be as physically strong as nonrecycled paper. Finally, batch variation would be expected given the changing nature of the starting materials that arrive at the recycling plant. With this in mind, differences among and between recycled paper batches would be expected:

- ✓ Microscopic and visual: color variation, shorter fibers
- ✓ Organic: residual contaminants and inks, de-inking materials such as soaps and pet ether, as examples
- ✓ Inorganic: de-inking materials such as hydroxides and buffer residues.

Source: Biermann, C. J. *Essentials of Pulping and Papermaking* San Diego, CA: Academic Press; 1993. Chapter 10: Fiber From Recycled Paper.

2. Predict how paper will appear under polarized light and justify.

Since paper contains cotton and other wood fibers, there should be areas that show interference colors, but these areas will be randomly dispersed throughout the matrix.

3. Show by calculation why aperture size is of more concern in IR than in UV/VIS. If an aperture size of 5 x 5µm is used to gather an IR spectrum, will diffraction likely occur? What about if this aperture size was used in the visible range?

The range of mid-infrared spectroscopy is ~100–4000 cm^{-1} wavenumbers. Converting to wavelengths yields:

$$v(cm^{-1}) = \frac{1}{\lambda(cm)} = \frac{10000\frac{\mu m}{cm}}{\lambda(\mu\mu m} \quad ; \quad \lambda(\mu\mu m = \frac{10000\frac{\mu m}{cm}}{v(cm^{-1})} ;$$

$$100\,cm^{-1} = 25\,\mu m \quad and \quad 4000\,cm^{-1} = 2.50\,\mu m$$

Diffraction effects increase as the aperture size approaches wavelength and so some diffraction effects would be expected with this example.